A BEGINNER'S GUIDE TO LIFE AFTER DEATH

The Teachings of Wilhelm & John
An Experience in Automatic Writing

BY
PETER SHIRES

Fortune Books Ltd

A FORTUNE BOOK
First Published in the UK 2000 by

FORTUNE BOOKS LTD
Sycamore House
Park Road
Colton, Leeds LS15 9AJ

Edited by Heather Pedley

Final editing assistance by Alice Walkingshaw
Cover illustration by David Coffey

Printed and bound in Great Britain by Bell and Bain Ltd

ISBN: 1-903782-00-7

For reasons of privacy,
some of the names in this book may have been changed.

For Maureen

A BEGINNER'S GUIDE
TO LIFE AFTER DEATH

The Teachings of Wilhelm & John
An Experience in Automatic Writing.

BY
PETER SHIRES

The Awakening

Three years ago I was an atheist - utter, complete, uncompromising. Now I have a knowledge (and I choose that word carefully, having considered the less dogmatic term 'belief'), which has completely reversed my conviction of more than 20 years that there was no life after death.

I did not have that conviction changed by a priest, bible or any orthodox religious persuasion. Almost by accident the door was opened for me and I peeped through the chink. I have an open mind and what I saw was interesting, indeed exciting. With trepidation and in the early stages with fear, I delved further. My curiosity overcame my fear and eventually I made what seemed to me to be an incredible discovery:

I am gifted with automatic writing. This means that friends (I can no longer refer to them as spirits) who have previously lived on Earth and are now considered dead, communicate by using me and in particular my hand, as an instrument for their thoughts and messages. I sit down with a pen and paper in front of me but I do not consciously write. My hand and the pen move apparently of their own volition but actually at the bidding of my colleagues, for I have come to consider them as such.

I generally write for 30 or 40 minutes, normally at a very rapid speed, without pause for thought or grammatical construction. But then I have no need for thought, because the thinking is done for me. I am merely a writing instrument, receiving and recording this communication. Later on I received this communication in the form of teachings, passed onto me by those who are most anxious to inform us of the simple truth.

Two of these fundamental truths are:

a) That life is eternal.

b)That the average Earth life of three score years and ten represents only a short excursion in trial and experience, in order that we might learn from such experiences and progress towards perfection in this eternal life.

There are people who will find nothing surprising in what I have written thus far. Provided they are convinced I am telling the truth they will consider it perfectly believable. Such people will recognise my experience as just one of the many phenomena experienced by thousands of other people, more usually in the form of clairvoyance or clairaudience. Such people would, I hope, read on from pure academic interest.

There are those, however, (undoubtedly the majority) who if they have managed to get past the third paragraph, have read this far out of mild curiosity and a sporting instinct, which allows even a 'nutcase' reasonable preface in which to develop an argument. Such people are generally called realists, pragmatists, often atheists. I have great affinity with them. Until recently my outlook and opinions were as theirs. I have special points of information I would like to impart, which are: that I have never been inside a spiritualist church, and have never been to a séance in the accepted sense. Moreover, in the last 25 years I have visited orthodox churches on no more than a dozen ceremonial occasions. I do not have visions nor do I go into a trance. I work hard in my business and cope well in this materialistic world, yet I have become utterly convinced that life after death is a fact. If you have an open mind then perhaps you will be inclined to read on, at least out of curiosity.

Obviously, it is reasonable to surmise that after living 37 years as an atheist, one does not just suddenly become aware that there is something more than the physical and material aspect to our world, without either studying or contemplating the subject, or perhaps through having some deep mental shock to the system. Yet I was not initiated by any such means.

Before proceeding with the automatic writings which developed into teachings from my friends on the other side of the etheric, I feel it is necessary to relate how I became interested in psychic phenomena and how as time progressed I discovered my own latent psychic ability and how it developed.

Up to the time when I discovered that I had the ability for automatic writing, I believed that I lived most of my life to a reasonably high ethical and moral standard, with what I considered to be the intellectual concepts of the average humanist. I believed then (and still do) that the basic law of right and wrong can be applied to most situations and common sense generally enlightened one as to what was right. I think my general outlook coincided with the moral framework of most of the religions of the world, without the usual ceremonial and symbolic trappings inherent in most religions, such being incomprehensible to me.

I had rarely visited church and quite frankly, had an almost unconscious opinion that the religions of the world had done mankind little service for the last 2,000 years, and they had little to offer myself by way of moral or spiritual inspiration.

I had always led a very active business and indeed social life without giving too much thought to death, or even old age. I suppose, were anyone to ask my opinion as to whether or not there was life hereafter and whether or not anything happened to the soul or spirit when we died, my opinion would have been doubtful. I simply did not believe in afterlife. I believed that mankind was an intellectual fluke in the animal kingdom - although I must confess I did not think deeply about the matter.

Then approximately three years ago, my wife Maureen, who had no profound views on the subject herself at the time, although I considered her to be somewhat more 'Christian' or religious than myself, began to tell me about a friend of hers called Betty. She claimed that Betty could heal - by placing her hands on a person in the peace and quiet of her own home. In many instances she could take away pain or remove or alleviate the symptoms and causes of various illnesses. Betty herself had been to a healer some years earlier and had been cured of a quite serious complaint. She subsequently developed the ability herself.

Betty was of course deemed to be a spiritualist and Maureen, although at that time still quite sceptical about the spiritual aspect of healing, stated categorically that she could not question the success. As time progressed and with more and more 'proof' of the healings, Maureen became more interested in the subject and read avidly the many books given to her by Betty. Most of the time I was totally oblivious to their interests, though I had an open mind on the subject, which had always been my tendency with such unexplained phenomena - neither believing nor disbelieving.

At the same time though, for some reason which I could not understand but can now more readily appreciate, I became more and more interested in various unexplained phenomena of a more scientific nature. I began to read books about ancient mysteries of the world and in particular numerous books on the subject of UFOs. Amongst all the data and evidence published on such subjects, I came to the conclusion that although science could neither prove or disprove, too many people were writing too many books about such matters for there not to be some possibility or 'essence' of truth in the various informed assertions. I began to wonder: Are people visiting us from other planets in the universe? Is thought transference possible? Do certain people have the power to move matter with their minds? and so on. It was not until around that time, however, that I ever considered that the 'spiritual' concept might have anything to do with some of the unexplained happenings and experiences going on in the world.

I read about Uri Geller and was transformed. I observed him on television and I believed him. I experienced frustration with the many scientists and magicians who were either trying to discredit him or reproduce his phenomena without opening their minds and examining exactly what was the cause of his extraordinary ability. Further, it seemed inconceivable that Dr Andrija Puharich, who had nurtured Geller through his experiences, should waste his time being involved in a fraud or in something which was not totally authentic as far as could be seen.

Throughout history scientists and 'experts' have ridiculed and decried what they could not prove by experiment, or renounced what they could not conceive of. Copernicus was persecuted for his theory that the world was round. And it was apparent to me, that our cultures and civilizations were still made up of these 'flat-earthers', people who were unprepared to explore the possibility of something more.

It seemed to me ridiculous that rational, highly intelligent and experienced civil airline pilots, entrusted to carry hundreds of people around the world in machinery costing millions of dollars, were treated like liars when they reported that unknown objects had flown along side of them and then disappeared vertically at fantastic speed. They were called 'fools', or thought of as being demented by the so-called 'experts' and authorities.

I found that I began to feel quite strongly about this. Although these stories sounded fantastic, surely it was more appropriate to simply wonder at these reported incidents, or accept the possibility that it just might be beyond our comprehension at our present stage of evolvement on earth.

I was not fully aware at that time that my mind was indeed opening and beginning to question such unexplainable material available in many unusual books, which I was reading thanks to my wife's friendship with Betty.

Maureen was and still is, an avid library goer. She gave me many interesting books and true life accounts to read and I was fascinated. I found it difficult to question these authors because I believed that their life experiences showed such sincerity. I read about Arigo, 'Surgeon of the Rusty Knife', Edward Chapman, the famous British healer and many other books too numerous to mention.

I was, however, not yet sufficiently interested to make a serious study of spiritualism. I was still much of a sceptic in this direction. I believed that 'something' was happening to the people who were psychic or had the ability to heal, but could not conceive that it was anything to do with life after death. Then came my first experience, which proved to me that I would have to examine this scepticism.

Betty suggested to Maureen that she and a friend come to our house one Saturday afternoon and attempt to record the psychic phenomenon of 'voices on tape'. She felt that as our house was a very old, warm and friendly abode, it would be the ideal setting for such an experiment. Maureen asked if I would mind and I said somewhat amusedly, that I had absolutely no objection. In any event, I would be watching television in another room whilst they were amusing themselves, so their foolishness could not possibly affect me.

They achieved no success with the recordings and after an hour or so they decided they would attempt to contact someone by the apparently well tried method of glass and letters, more commonly known as the 'Ouija Board'. When I popped through into the other room and saw what they were doing I thought they had taken leave of their senses. However, they seemed to be enjoying themselves, so I indulgently and amusedly stood by the table and watched them.

The glass was in fact moving about the table and spelling letters and the communicator was supposedly a person called 'Jack'. Various letters were being spelt out although the ladies were not able to decipher or understand them. Yet I had to confess something did appear to be happening. They were all honest people and quite serious about what they were doing and I wasn't prepared to believe that they were in fact manipulating the glass themselves. My open mind led me to believe that perhaps something was really going on. It was at this point I think, that I realised my curiosity had only been thinly veiled.

The messages coming through were making no sense at all to either Betty or my wife and yet the communicator, Jack, was insisting that he was part of our family. My wife couldn't place him at all and so the questions continued. Then suddenly I began to have a deep, fearful feeling. I recognised the person, or rather the contents of the communications indicated to me that the person talking was actually my grandfather, who had been dead for more than 25 years.

My wife had never known him and the name 'Jack' meant nothing to her. The message that was coming through said that he was 'Ernest called Jack'. This statement was a total mystery to Maureen but not to me, for though my grandfather's name had indeed been 'Ernest', his contemporaries knew him as 'Jack'. Similarly, my own father, who was christened 'John', has been known throughout his life as 'Jack'.

This little spark of information completely opened my mind to questioning and so I did. I was standing several feet away from the table and I asked him through the ladies if he would prove to me who he was, by relating family circumstances and family names which would be unknown to any other person in that room. This he did in no uncertain manner and

I was both amazed and bewildered, because at no time did I myself place my fingers on the glass.

The numerous names and incidents which my grandfather related to me convinced me utterly that it was actually he who was communicating. In particular, incidents relating to his employment many years ago which my father later verified were most convincing. What was more, even the tone of the messages and the humour contained in the communications was typical and most characteristic of my grandfather's own particular brand of humour. I felt I could actually recognise his personality through the messages.

This experience intrigued me sufficiently enough to pursue the study of the spiritual concept more seriously. Both myself, my wife and one or two other family members attempted with success to communicate through the glass. We contacted all sorts of people, of varying degrees of intellect. Most of them gave messages which were unverifiable, but nevertheless so unrelated in content to our own thoughts and knowledge, that we couldn't rationally explain it. By this time we were all convinced that these messages were indeed coming from people who had 'passed on' previously. The fact that it was the family taking part in these communication sessions was a personal safeguard to ensure that no one was attempting to deceive by consciously or purposefully moving the glass.

In these early days I was totally without fear and in ignorance of any possible harmful effects which might come to me or my family through our preoccupation with contacting the 'other side'. My reasoning was that surely nothing which could not harm me if I was oblivious to it could possibly harm me if I was aware of it and yet I feel I must here introduce a serious word of caution to any uninitiated person who might be reading this.

I did not realise that in operating the glass and letters, we were in fact acting in a primitive manner as mediums or 'channels' for spirits or entities on the 'other side'. I have since learned that there is great debate as to the advisability of people pursuing such pastimes in ignorance and without benefit of advice from serious and developed mediums. I personally received guidance on this afterwards and I will come back to this subject later.

After a few weeks of very interesting and varied communications with many people, we found that two particular individuals came through to us most of the time. One was 'Wilhelm' and the other was 'John'. They stated they were brothers on the other side of the etheric. A third person whose name was 'Jack' also used to come through, usually on a Sunday if my brother Nicholas was present. (This was a different 'Jack' to my grandfather.) He stated that he had particular affinity with my brother. From around that time we had no communication with any other people but these three and most of my contact from then on was with Wilhelm and John.

I say 'my' contact, because I very quickly learned that with a little contemplation and practice I could eventually move the glass by myself with no need for anyone else to be present and I found myself following this pursuit at many odd moments during the week when I felt I had the time. Indeed, I used to practice this occasionally at my office during lunchtime, usually one day a week, with two colleagues who were also interested in the subject.

As time progressed I detected clearly a difference in intellect between my two friends Wilhelm and John and in the early stages there seemed to be a battle of interests between them as to who would communicate with me. I felt that many of the messages from John in those early days were somewhat inane and childish, as though coming from a person of lower intellect. At times I even became alarmed at the content of the messages. It was as though John was a mischievous person, not always concerned with giving the correct advice and guidance, but more interested in creating sensation and alarm. The messages from Wilhelm and the level of intelligence indicated in his communications were of a much higher nature. For a time, Wilhelm strongly advised me not to have any further communications with John and I followed this advice.

I found the glass moved more strongly with John than with Wilhelm, however, and that when I wished to communicate with Wilhelm, John could dominate the process and interfere. However, Wilhelm must have had an influence in restraining him from making contact because eventually Wilhelm came to be the dominant figure.

Wilhelm explained this to me at the time. He told me that John was of relatively low intellect, but although he could be a little mischievous at times, he actually meant no harm. He was merely over-joyed at having the ability to make contact with me and was more or less indulging himself with a new occupation.

I was also told that this particular phenomenon and Wilhelm's communication had a more serious intent to it. He bid me to communicate only with him for the time being, once a week when he would be available. He asked me not to talk to John in the meantime, until he gave his permission, for reasons that would be made clear to me at a later date. Because of the obvious difference in intellect, I took notice of Wilhelm.

I had many discussions through the glass with Wilhelm, whereby he introduced me to and taught me more about the concept of afterlife and indeed the concept of universal life and after a while he gradually allowed John to talk to me in between these instructions. Though the content in John's messages was still not very profound we appeared, however, to build up a very interesting and friendly relationship. I think in those early days he must have somehow 'fed' off my fear because as my fear lessened he ceased to relate alarming gibberish.

So, almost by accident, this is how I became aware of life after death. Never at any time did there appear to me to be anything 'occult' or even mysterious about the subject. Once I had lost my early fear, which I now understand is caused by ignorance and is the natural reaction of any uninitiated person in this very materialistic and sceptical world, and once I had become able to accept and believe in the phenomenon, I found that my progression was rapid.

The culmination was my discovering that, just as I could place my hand on the glass and allow it through a will other than my own to move about the table spelling out letters of the alphabet, so could I hold a pen loosely in my hand and allow it to write, apparently of its own volition.

Again it was precipitated almost by accident

and at the time of discovery I 'kicked' myself for not having attempted it before, for logic suggested it must be possible! If a glass could move, then why not a pen?

My wife had been reading a book written through an automatic writer and it was she who suggested I try it. I had also read about Matthew Manning and his extraordinary psychic artistry and medical diagnosis, so I did not hesitate at my wife's suggestion. When I contacted John through the glass I could almost feel his excitement as he bid me to try using a pen.

What follows is the result of a tentative exercise between John and myself, with the half-hope between us that it would work and he would manage to communicate. We were not disappointed. . . .

The First Writings

23rd March

I held the pen loosely in my hand and I attempted to empty my mind. In a few moments the pen started to move all over the page, scribbling backwards and forwards, up and down at random. Gradually after more and more excited and almost frantic exercise, my hand steadied and I knew that the time had come to attempt to form words. I started a new page and the following words came through from John:

Believe me you can do it. You can do anything you wish.

I asked him one or two questions of no significance simply for the exercise and received a scrawled reply. I then asked him if Wilhelm was with him. He replied:

No, he is away.

As Wilhelm had not been around for some time I asked if he would be coming back soon . John replied:

Yes, in two weeks.

I asked him further insignificant questions, simply

because I was largely lost for words in the midst of this experience, but he seemed then to take the initiative and said:

You have to try more things like this. Yes, yes, you are protected, you protect yourself. *(He appeared to be reading the fear in my mind.)* You are high plane. Yes you can do many things.

In answer to various other questions he replied:

Yes, yes you should expect more from yourself. Yes, you can do more with your life. You are very spiritual. Yes, you should. . .

The writing tailed away. I asked him if he was tired and he replied:

Yes.

I asked him if it had been a great exertion for him and he replied:

Yes.

It was obvious to me that he could not continue any longer. The communication ceased.

26th March

The communications between John and myself continued a couple of days later.

You are very happy because you have the power to do this. You can do more. You should try to do other things. You should try to see me. You can do it by opening the other eye. You must try to do it.

You understand I am still afraid.

You must not be afraid, you will see many things. You will see the light of creation. You are gifted with much power but you are not aware of it. You could have many experiences, which will help you understand.

You begin by meditation and you let your mind wander and then you eventually see the light. The light is very great and it eventually sets you into the other world.

You will see me and you will see Wilhelm and other people who are on this side. You will be aware that you are with us but still on Earth. You will not see anything bad because there is nothing bad. There is nothing to fear because you are protected and you protect yourself. You are not ignorant in the etheric, you only think you are because you are unaware.

You will see many things which you would not believe, you will become aware of what life is really about.

Will I leave my body?

No, you will not leave your body, You will only see.

Will I see in the same way as Betty?

No, Betty does not have the power that you have. Yours is more perceptive.

Are some of these writings my own thoughts, am I expressing my own subconscious feelings?

These are all my thoughts, you have done none of this. Betty sees but she does not understand what she sees. You would see us and understand more fully. Yes, you will see the same way but understand more. It has taken a long time for your spiritual awareness to open but it has always been there. You have had the gift always but did not know. Do not be afraid, try it tonight. I will look after you.

You have conquered fear before, you can overcome fear better than most. You will love the experience once you lose your fear.

Now that I have gained this ability is there a danger that I will become too preoccupied with such matters? I feel this is happening now.

No, you are preoccupied because of the new experience. Soon this will ease and you will live normally with the knowledge, but you have to extend your knowledge.

Are you able to move the pen and write with anyone else?

No, I can only move it with you because we have affinity together. Many lives and much time have elapsed between us. I have been with you for a long time, it is my life to be with you, my atonement.

Wilhelm was afraid my low intellect would misguide you, but now he knows you are on the right path and that you understand. Wilhelm did not wish to frighten you and he insisted he guide you, until he was sure. Now I am allowed and it gives me much pleasure to be trusted to such a matter.

You have stated previously that I am helping you, can you explain this further?

Yes you are helping me. My love for you is coming through. My karma is being helped. All my love and work is being fulfilled. I am very happy.

At this stage my wife Maureen was sitting close to me with a pen in her hand and felt that the pen was moving. She felt that she was having some success. I asked John if this was so and he replied:

She is having some success.

I asked who was helping her and if she should continue. He replied:

A friend of mine, but she should not do it, she is not yet protected.

My wife asked what was the message she was receiving, as the writing was hardly discernible. He replied:

The message was from her father. He wants her to know that he is happy.

John detected my fears and continued:

You are right to be frightened. Maureen must not do this. She is not protected. Yes the friend is good but he will not always be there. Maureen has had bad experience, she is not yet ready. Her mind is not ready and she could be harmed by the wrong people. Tell her to stop now and never try again until Wilhelm says she may. Now stop.

He was telling her not to do it until she is aware. She must give herself time to develop. A friend was trying to stop her before she really starts. We are all good people around you but if Maureen does this when alone, or when we are not here, she might have bad experience. We love her and will tell you when she can do this.

She must get her mind good. She must recover from her father. She must be more positive and happy. She is worried, she has fears, she gets depressed. When she is lifted up and very happy we will let her progress. She has plenty of time, tell her not to hurry. She still has too many doubts. You cannot attempt such things until all doubts are gone.

You are more progressed than Maureen, you have nothing to fear. Maureen has been hurt in previous lives, she has suffered much. She is healing in this life. She is being opened up in this life to awareness. She has been deprived previously and now she is having reward by a happy life and a good family, but her deep instinct will not let her fully believe. She is a pessimist from past lives and she expects the worst. That is why she worries. She cannot believe tomorrow will be as good as today.

Nothing matters except love. Money is nothing, possessions are nothing, only love. Maureen has much love to give. She should give it and take it and not worry. Help her believe in the future, nothing matters except love. Help her be optimistic, you know this. Then she will develop and be very happy. She is very secure with you and in any event is well loved here.

You will understand love fully when you die. Rejoice for the dead for they have arrived home. The biggest problem for the dead is worrying about loved ones left on Earth. They have pain in trying to reach them and tell their family that everything here is happiness. If their family were able to understand they would rejoice for them.

Try to help Maureen accept this. She must not forget her father but when she remembers she should think of how happy he is and not that he is lost to her.

I then asked if my wife had psychic ability. John replied:

Yes, Maureen has powers and she has already tried them. She has experimented but she is not ready. Her mind enquires but it is not yet ready. She still suffers wounds from previous lives and fear has no place in experiments. The mind and intellect must be crystal clear, this gives protection.

Fear is at the root of all evil. It causes illness, it causes badness, war, disease, trouble. If there were no fear then the world would be beautiful, but conquering fear has to be learned. You have spent many lives conquering fear and now you have no fear, even though you think you have. Your lack of fear gets you into trouble but it also protects you. Lack of fear and love go together, because only through love can you conquer fear.

Love sweeps fear aside, but you must on earth also apply common sense. Because of systems and conventions and other people, you have to conform a little in order to survive. You have often, through fearlessness, forgot common sense but you are learning fast. You are now joining your fearlessness together with your love and common sense and beginning to acquire more wisdom. We enjoy watching you progress. It is fun to us.

When you get over here you will laugh at the many things you did, but you will not be ashamed. Your Karma has progressed and you can be happy with your life. People who hate and who do bad things are full of sorrow when they come over and their Karma suffers.

Spread love around, make people happy in small ways. If you are happy the light shines through. It is like medicine to other people.

You can heal with happiness. Love and light make people forget pain. There is too much pain in the world. It makes us sad that people do not know how easy life could be with total love. There is enough of what is needed for all. The joys of life are simple when tried.

Helping unfortunates is inspiring and makes the helpers more happy. It is as the nourishment of nectar, to love people from the heart, just because the love is there in the heart.

These words are our simple way of expressing the truths. You are now fortunate to have such knowledge. I believe you will spend the rest of your life applying these truths. You should be very happy.

I then asked if I had improved since I had become 'enlightened'.

Yes, since you became aware of the truth you have improved a great deal and you will get better. You are fortunate to acquire this knowledge during earth life because it will save you centuries of incarnation in learning. You will become a better person and you will die a very good person. How can it be otherwise now? You have the ultimate knowledge on Earth. Can you cheat, can you hurt, can you do wrong to others now that you are aware of the effect on your Karma? No, you cannot and you are lucky to know this.

At this stage I became aware that the writings were much more profound than is normal with John and I asked if John was still speaking. I received the following reply:

No, this is Wilhelm. Yes, it is Wilhelm. Yes, John is loving you. I am very proud of John. His intellect is limited but his love is pure. Yes it is me. Yes and I have missed you but I have been very busy with people much worse-off than you. I am kept very busy. You can write with me once a week each Friday from now on, but you can also write with John between. John has passed his apprenticeship. He has brought you out. Love him he is your brother. We are triumvirate and triumphant together.

I then asked Wilhelm when he had started to write.

I started to write at the beginning. John told me what had happened between you and I came as soon as I could.

I asked Wilhelm why this writing had not been possible before.

You never tried it before and we did not know we would have the power. Don't be afraid now, we have taken you along slowly, but now you are developing fast. Now you must meditate and you will see us. I am going now, I will come next Friday. I am very tired now with the effort.

I love you all, bless all, Wilhelm.

27th March

The following day I was persuaded by my daughter to again demonstrate the phenomenon. I could not resist and received this short but encouraging message from John.

You are very happy to do this, you are very excited about this.

My wife had also requested that I ask how her mother was accepting the recent death of her father.

Yes, she is aware that Bob is happy. Bob is trying to let her know that he is alright.

In answer to my enquiry if my father-in-law was 'near' he replied:

No he is away at the moment and resting. He will come soon. He is happy that you are spiritual, it helps him because he does not worry. Most people who die worry about the people whom they leave behind because most people grieve and do not believe. Your family all believe and it helps Bob.

I then asked John to confirm that it was Wilhelm communicating with me last night.

Yes, it was Wilhelm last night. He will come once a week and I will talk to you in between.

To my further questions he answered:

Yes, you should write a book and let others know about this. You must spread the light wherever possible. We on this side wish people to be aware of the truth and people like you are messengers. You can spread the message for us.

I asked him if he had any particular message to pass on at the moment.

No, the only message is love to all. You are now on a true and exciting path. You are very fortunate to have this ability. Make much of your life from now on.

28th March

John opened the conversation with personal messages and encouragement to do with business. In particular he referred to a good idea I had had.

I asked him if it was purely mine or had he had a hand in it. He stated that it was my own thought but he had helped me nurture it.

I then told him that occasionally I felt I was confusing thoughts which originated in my mind with thoughts which came from him.

Yes, but with practice you will know all the time. Yes, you will become more perceptive.

I then asked him if he could move the pen through anyone else. He replied:

No, I can only move it through you.

I then said I would attempt to clear my mind completely of thought to see what happened. He replied:

You cannot empty your mind because I keep putting ideas there.

I was in fact experimenting with my thoughts and my mind because I was always having doubts. I told him

31

that I could not help having doubts and feeling that my subconscious was moving the pen.

No, you must not have doubts, you really know in your heart that it is true.

I said that I understood, that generally speaking with automatic writing the style of writing sometimes tended to be in the style of communicator and not the writer but these writings were in my hand, or close to my hand, even though the speed of input caused me to scribble.

Yes, it is because your personality is very strong. You cannot be fully manipulated. All I can do is put the thoughts through and guide your hand, I cannot manipulate you further.

I detected he had struggled to find the word 'manipulate' and I pointed out that I had purposely and consciously not helped when he hesitated. He said:

Yes, you could have helped but you did not want to lead me. It is best that you have this approach then it will be more convincing and settle your doubts.

I then asked him if it was he who had communicated the last time. I had felt for some time now that Wilhelm couldn't communicate directly with me, but that he used John as a channel.

It was me. No, Wilhelm cannot do so, he uses me as an instrument to you.

I asked him if Wilhelm would come through next Friday as arranged.

Yes, Wilhelm will instruct me what to say and I pass it on. Wilhelm has not the power. I have the power because I have been close to you all my life. I think like you, you are my mentor.

I expressed surprise at this and said that he spoke as though I was teaching him.

Yes, you are my guide. I was put with you to learn.

At that moment there was some very noisy gun shooting on the television which distracted me and I said almost in passing, 'Can you hear those awful violent people?' He replied immediately: 'Yes, but only through your mind, your thoughts . . .' *and continued with the writing.*

It was surprising to me how quickly we were developing along casual conversation lines, almost as though we were sitting talking to each other rather than writing. He continued:

The power thinks it better that I have a guide on Earth. Now I can learn by your mistakes and difficulties and by observing how you overcome them.

Surely you have difficulties over there?

Yes we do, but they are different. We do not face the same trials. We can live a soft life if we wish but we do not then progress. I am learning how to face and overcome problems with you, then I will come down and try again. I hope I am as successful as you.

I then told him that his thoughts were hitting my mind a fraction of a second before the pen moved. In other words, the communication was getting stronger and stronger. Also my wife who was with us pointed out that she herself picked up the thoughts before the pen wrote them down.

Yes, Maureen is sitting close and is picking up the vibrations. I am transferring my thoughts to you but it is like music to the spiritual ear. It can be picked up by others, especially Maureen because she is psychic.

Maureen then said she felt very distant as though she might go into a trance. I asked him if this was possible.

Yes, it could happen. She should move away now.

Can you read Maureen's thoughts?

I cannot read Maureen's thoughts. She can pick up mine because she can receive, but I cannot receive because Maureen does not have the power or development to transmit.

I asked why he could pick up mine but not Maureen's.

I can pick up yours because you and I have affinity.

Maureen remarked that it did not make sense and I passed this on. He replied:

Yes it does, when you fully understand. It is

difficult to explain. We can only pick up certain thoughts from people who have affinity with us.

I asked him about Wilhelm and he replied:

Wilhelm can only pick up yours.

We then asked him if anyone could pick up Maureen's thoughts.

Yes her father can because he is still close to her.

We then asked if Maureen had a guide and he replied:

Yes, she has a guide but guides do not communicate in such manner.

We asked if there was anyone there who could pick up her thoughts.

No not here. Only her father when he is around. He is away being taught and resting. He will be back soon.

Maureen then asked if when she prayed her thoughts were not received.

Yes, of course they are received, but not by people as low as me. They are received by high-level spirits who then instruct guides and helpers to give assistance.

I then asked jokingly if he needed his own prayers answering occasionally.

Yes, that is true. People like me are often more in need than people like Maureen.

Maureen had felt her father's presence a few days ago and I asked John about this.

Yes, he was standing behind Maureen. I was with him all evening. Yes, he comes regularly. Yes, he spends more time with (her mother) Annie than with Maureen, which is only natural.

I asked if Bob had settled down. He replied:

Yes, very quickly.

After discussions with my wife, I asked John if we could experiment by her pointing to figures and him transmitting them back through my mind.

No. It is not my business to prove the fact by

experiments, there has to be trust and belief. Things cannot be made easy for you. The whole of religious teaching is based on faith and love. If we were to spend our time proving through clever tricks there would be no point in coming to earth to develop faith. Everybody would have the knowledge too quickly. Each has to be enlightened through his or her own effort.

Maureen pointed out that Jesus gave proof. He replied:

That was a special event and special circumstances. He set the faith for all to follow. Love, nothing but love. Unfortunately the religious dogmatists have distorted his truths and the modern world demands proof. We cannot and it is not in people's interest to give proof, otherwise the whole of life on Earth is a waste of time.

We then asked if he could tell us something about Uri Geller.

Uri is a highly developed medium. Uri is like you but more developed. This gift is given to few people, people who have earned it. You have worked for the knowledge through your karma. It has taken thousands of years for you to reach this state of awareness. You are an old spirit.

We asked if he could only speak through me or could he speak through anyone. He replied:

No, neither of us has the power. No, I do not have the power.

I then detected he was tired and asked if he wished to leave. He replied 'Yes'. Maureen asked through me if he could leave her with a special message before he went. He replied:

Be prepared to believe without proof. We cannot buy your faith, it has to be given. Once we know we have your belief then proof will follow but by such time you will not require such proof because the knowledge will be within you. Peter has acquired this knowledge with his open mind. It does not matter to him now who else believes, he himself knows the truth. Goodnight.

I had had the feeling for some time that some of the thoughts coming through were those of Wilhelm. I asked if Wilhelm was there. He replied:

Yes, Wilhelm is here.

I then kept him a little while longer and asked if anyone else would ever write through me. He replied:

No, only Wilhelm and I will come through because we have affinity with you.

I then pressed him and asked if it were not possible in the future, if someone had a particular message to transmit and he said:

It is possible, we will have to wait and see.

I pressed further, I had in mind Matthew Manning and the sort of writings which were received by him and I asked if he knew of Matthew Manning.

Yes, we understand what you are seeking but you must wait. Wilhelm has much to say to you and you must first learn about yourself. Our first duty is to teach you, then we will see how you develop from there.

Love and bless you all.

The Teachings

1st April

We have now reached the stage whereby I fully accept the phenomenon. Until this time most of the writings had been in the form of questions and answers and mostly with John, without too much concern with the content of the writings.

The following is the first promised communication from Wilhelm through John, whereby he would begin what he had termed, 'my instruction'. It did however start with quite a lengthy discourse on personal problems and I received a substantial amount of advice. After this they asked me to pause and come back to it in about ten minutes. His actual words were:

Yes, have a rest and get it out of your mind and come back. We do not want sordid Earth thoughts in your mind from now on. Come back in a while.

When I returned he continued:

Yes, here you are again. You should empty all earth thoughts from your mind. We are going to begin your teaching. Are you ready?

In answer to my request that my daughter, who was present, could remain, he replied:

Yes of course, she is welcome.

The first thing for you to understand is the law of Karma. This is the most difficult principle for people of your life to grasp and understand. You have to work your karma through for eons of time. Beginning as a very low form of organism and repeatedly reincarnating up through the spheres of existence.

The stage you are now at is very advanced. You have made many mistakes through centuries of living on Earth. First as a mere organism and then on through low animal form. The first major step in development was your incarnation into man, albeit low intelligence man at first. Then you progressed through innumerable lives on Earth to your present stage.

Between all these human lives on Earth you came home to our world and you rested and reflected on how your life had been used. Sometimes you were disappointed because you had wasted your opportunity and at others you were quite pleased. Each time you learned something about the only thing that matters in development through the spheres. You learned about love. The power of love is infinite. It is the law which governs all other laws.

Let us go back a little, we are running too fast.

I felt that because I was attempting to write slowly and legibly I was losing the thoughts and I remarked on this.

Yes, it is better that you write quickly. Sometimes we lose the thread and cannot get thoughts through to you. Clear your mind, let it flow. Stop looking and it will come through.

Whilst you were in 'our world' you also learned by attaching yourself to higher forms than you. People like Wilhelm taught you through his love and you reflected on other people's actions on Earth. By such means you could see the benefit to karma of love in relationships and also the damage caused by bad thoughts and deeds.

Bad thoughts and deeds are terrible for karma and for advancement. Love is white, advancement, light, heat, healing, goodness. Evil is darkness, illness, sorrow. Light attracts light. Love people and they love you, even though this is not immediately apparent. Help and you are helped. Give and all is given. Hurt people and you receive like kind. Think black and evil and such will come to you. Trouble and bad thoughts cause illness of spirit and can actually cause illness of the physical body. The spirit reacts on the body. Love cleanses the mind and the mind cleanses the body.

This is the whole truth about spiritual healing. Not all people who visit spiritual healers are made well. Only when those people display open, trusting, loving countenance and pure good will, this together with love and the good will of the healers (because they cannot heal without it), then the physical illness can be cured. Even cancers, even lost causes.

This is effected from our side. Sometimes we will help some sick body to be healed because we know it will be good for their spirit. If only (in many cases) the ill person knew that their spirit affects their physical body, we would not need to bother. But as they generally do not, we have to reverse the procedure and heal the body to effect the purification of the spirit. For whomsoever receives a so-called 'miracle of healing', must be sufficiently impressed of the spiritual process to receive some benefit for the rest of their Earth lives. Generally they become better persons on Earth because of healing and tend to thank their blessings from then on.

This improves the spirit so that they can think more of other people and help other people, if only with a smile. Such improvement generally improves the karma and then they return to us more educated, with their 'three score years and ten' not wasted.

I then asked if I could pause to get a cigarette. He replied:

Yes, get yourself a cigarette you fool.

We continued.

So this is some insight into karma. You cannot comprehend how long it takes to work through to a very high plane, but nevertheless you are almost there. It is doubtful that you will again come to Earth, unless you throw away the rest of your life - especially now that you are receiving this teaching.

You are fortunate - one of very few - who actually become truly spiritually aware whilst on Earth. This has nothing to do with orthodox religion. Many people who think they are spiritually aware are not. They study the Bible and other distortions of man and in a vain and pious way they go through the motions of doing good for the world, but deep down it lacks sincerity (not all you understand, some church people are of very high karma). But they cannot hide their thoughts from the teachers on this side, nor from themselves, for they in fact are the final judge of their actions when they again reach this side.

No, they cannot hide from this, because all is eventually revealed and when they come over they realise that it does not matter how many candles they lit, nor how many prayers they said. What matters is how did they feel as they proceeded through their earthly life? How did their deep mind react to people and situations? Did they really love their fellow man? Did they really cry in their heart when they saw suffering or were they 'crocodile tears' just from the eyes? Because it is how the heart feels, (really it is the mind) and it cannot be hidden. You can put a cloak over your face and hide your feelings, but you cannot hide your innermost feelings from yourself. Nor from us.

Every emotion is registered around your spiritual body and around your earth body. This can be seen by some gifted people on Earth and is called 'Aura'. Your Aura reflects everything about you. It attracts or repels you from evil and love. If you have angry emotions your Aura changes whilst the anger lasts. If you have loving emotions then likewise your Aura reflects that love.

Sometimes people on Earth can pick up these emotions. This is the second sense you talk about when you instantly dislike someone, or when you know someone dislikes you even though they might be smiling. These emotions can usually be hidden on Earth by self-controlled people, but it is impossible to hide the Aura in the etheric.

In addition to these changing emotions - they can change from day to day, or moment-by-moment depending on the state of the mind - there are permanent imprints of the personality contained in the Aura. From here we can read love, happiness and benignness in people, just as we can read evil and negative personalities. We only have to 'see' a person to know their mentality.

But the Aura can change as the person improves. This is the karma working through and it takes eons and many lives to achieve a good Aura. It has to be learned in the school of life. A person's Aura can noticeably improve throughout earth life if their thoughts and instincts are improving, if their love is overcoming evil. Also, the Aura can deteriorate if the reverse is true.

I think we have explained enough tonight for you to digest. Your Aura is now advanced and it is getting better as the thoughts in your head improve. We said previously that you should not find it necessary to come to Earth again because over the centuries you have evolved sufficiently to leave the planes which are near to Earth - then your teaching really starts and it is something to look forward to.

One thing! Never look down on, nor indeed despair for people who are on a lower plane. You have been there and have had the experience to lift you. You have earned your place and they will earn theirs. It is absolutely necessary for them to experience in order to advance. In fact there is just no other way to advance but through many lives and experiences. It is the law which governs all laws. The progression to love and understanding, despite trial and adversity, demonstrated by Christ in the extreme, as an example to follow.

We want to stop but you thirst for knowledge. Your mind will not let us stop and John is very tired. We will just tell you a little more about John.

John is one of the beings whose advancement lags behind yours. He loves you because of your Aura and he bathes in your Aura. He wishes to reach your stage of advancement and he knows he must experience and live more lives on Earth to achieve this. This is why he is close to you on Earth. He lives his daily life with you. He learns how you tackle your problems. He reflects on how you react to situations and people. He tries to attune his thinking with yours. You teach him with your love and feelings.

If you became evil we would take John away from you because he is there to learn love and not evil. A person (we are not spirits), is only put to learn from someone who is more advanced. John is advanced more than others and he can teach people over here, but you are further along the path and he can learn much from you. Love John because he is now with you for life (unless you go bad and you won't). We leave him with you for the rest of your Earth life.

He will learn and progress and then when you die and come over he will be waiting, together with

Wilhelm. John will help you come over and help you rest back into the new awareness of this side. Then when you are ready, you will go on to your next progression and John will return to Earth, to live again the problems incurred on the Earth plane. Hopefully his subconscious will retain the love between you and he will retain some of the instinct learned. Perhaps you will help him from this side and guide him whilst he is there.

Love him, he is in your trust. Only hate from you can damage his karma whilst he is around you. We do not wish his karma to be damaged. Continue with this trust.

John is really very tired, we will talk next week.

Love from all, John, Wilhelm, Jack and friends.

2nd April

After one or two personal messages and short discourse from John, I asked him if he felt it would be possible for us to attempt automatic sketching. He said it would be possible to try though he stressed that he himself had no particular artistic talent.

I also am a worse-than-average artist but in a light-hearted frame of mind I decided with John to begin to see what would happen.

First achievements were very simple drawings of a boat and little girl. I then asked him if he would attempt to sketch himself in the guise of his last life on Earth. He seemed very keen.

The sketching took approximately an hour and I was very pleased with the result. The artwork was of a standard far higher than I personally have ever achieved and during the time of the sketching he was constantly making notes on the side of the drawing, advising me to rub out various parts of the anatomy and try again until we got it right.

In the end we achieved a reasonable sketch of him which we both felt was better than we could have hoped and with which we were very pleased. Afterwards he answered some questions about himself in that life. I remarked that he had sketched himself with a beard and asked if he had a beard now. He replied:

No, we are clean shaven now, hair only grows on humans. We can create any image we wish but Wilhelm will explain this in the future. I just draw for you my last appearance on the Earth plane.

Yes, I was rich and so were you. This is the dress of higher class. We had power and money in that life but it was not good for us. I was very bad. You were better but even you had faults in that life. You have since overcome but you were anyway much more advanced than I was. Now that I am beginning to advance, I hope in the next life, I will be a very good person. I am trying to prepare for the next incarnation.

Our relationship (in this past life) was friends of power and influence. Wilhelm was your brother. He tried to lead you on the correct path but I prevented him. I had wrong influence over you at that time. I was cruel and bad to people in my care. Your deep instinct was good but you were under my influence. Yes, I was a few years older than you. Wilhelm was your older brother. He was a doctor and philosopher, a very learned and good man.

I asked him for further details of myself.

I am not allowed to give any details, it is not my responsibility. Perhaps sometime Wilhelm will allow it but it is not really important for you to know. If I gave you such details you might be able to trace our ancestry, but they do not think you are ready to know. They do not think it wise at this stage. I would like to tell you but do not press me because I am now under your influence and would do as you bid, but I have to take notice of my teachers and the trust they put in me.

I want to tell you everything at once but they plan it all out and tell you a little each time so you will not be afraid or disbelieve. You understand, I know.

I asked him if he was allowed to tell me about any of his previous incarnations.

Yes I am allowed to tell that. Previously I lived in early England. Yes, about Middle Ages. I believe it was eleventh century. It is now so long the memory dims.

I was not important, only a peasant, very poor. Life was very hard, we were no better than slaves. Masters were very cruel and there were constant wars. People killed for no reason and tortured. Life was too cheap. I did not have a happy life and I was very ignorant. Perhaps that is why I was given a rich life last time, but I wasted it.

Next time I would like to be neither rich nor poor but I would like to achieve some good by my own efforts. Even if I was a carpenter I would like to be a very good one and have a loving wife and family. I want to give the love that I now have to a family and friends. I yearn to come back and gain new experience. I must climb to your level. I now see the light.

We must close now I am tired.

Goodnight and love. I will not be far away, John.

I am not surprised he was tired. We had spent something like two hours sketching and writing and only days had elapsed since the first five minutes of writing had caused him to stop with strain. We were apparently progressing very well. (See illustrations page 57, 58).

4th April

John started with a short message.

Hello, it is nice to talk to you. Love is the message. You are a little down today.

I had the beginning of a cold and had been unwell.

Yes you have worked hard, you should have a rest.

Once again we sketched for approximately an hour or less. Frequently the sketching was instructed by his writings with advice to me to rub out certain parts of the anatomy and re-attempt to sketch it correctly. I never ceased to be surprised at the various small details of the attire and the fact that they were not of my imagination.

The figure which emerged was that of a politician of the Middle Ages carrying a staff of office. This was apparently how I had looked. (See illustrations page 57, 58).

His comments on the sketch were as follows.

Yes, your dress was quite plain. Its colour was purple with green or grey hose. The staff was a mark of office. You were a chancellor and the staff was a chancellor's staff of office.

I asked him for further details and he replied:

I am still not allowed to say too much.

John 1535
France.

No my nose was not
so pointed
but it is quite good.

Yes if we do
more it will
be spoiled

Yes good legs

Yes
rub out the
legs they are
wrong. the face
is very good I am
better artist than
I thought

I shaded front on
but I have gone side
on. I think we go
side on

I am bad artist
I can't do legs
forget the legs
I cannot do hands
so we will clasp
them

Rub out legs
we try again.

No not see no more
I am not allowed
to say

No not hose
yes one more try

57

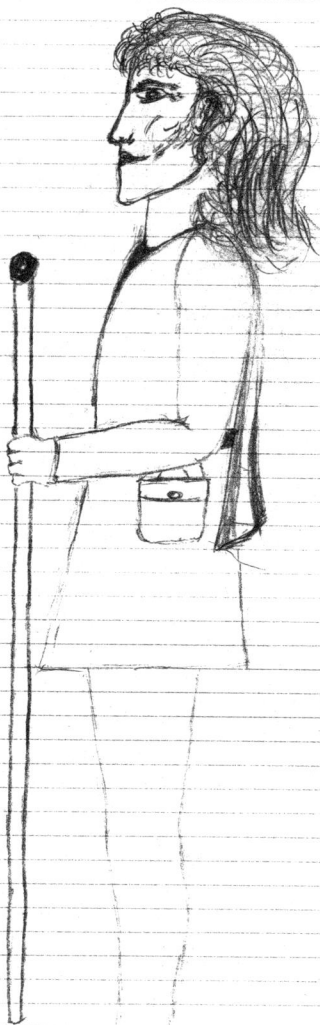

Rubb out nose
Rubb out chin
"   "   mouth
—   chin
stop nose
top nose
on near enough
we not perfect
yes the jaw is too
big rubb out jawline
No beard   you
yes   yes it an
yes

the Staff was your
indication of political
office. Your face was
not so fat more like
it is now. You then
beard? Yes we tidied
up later. Yes I
cannot get it too right
No too happy. It should be
thinner. Rubb out nose
first. Rubb out eyes Oh.
yes you can leave it
to me. No mean eyeball
Face is oh really if we
good enough artists.

That is OK NO more

58

8th April

Friday had come around again and as promised Wilhelm was present with John.

You are not very well today. Your Aura is poor. You need to rest and make yourself better before we can proceed with the teaching.

I had developed either a mild dose of flu or a bad cold, I wasn't quite sure which. I asked if Wilhelm was there, as all his writings apparently came through John to me.

Yes, Wilhelm is here but he does not wish to teach until you are well. No, you will be well in a few days. It is Earth flu but it is brought on by over-exertion. You have been very busy and you have pushed yourself too much last week. When this happens and there are viruses about the resistance is low. It is a normal happening.

People on Earth do not realise that rest is very important. Even if you work with your mind, your body becomes tired. You must rest your mind and body more. You know how to rest your body, you can learn to rest your mind through meditation. This cures and heals the mind. Banish all business and Earth problems away more regularly and contemplate. It will help you stay healthy.

Yes we write for a while but nothing profound. We need your intellect for profound teaching but your intellect is tired and we do not wish to tire you more until you are well. We will talk of light things.

You should be happy with your daughter. She is very spiritual and sympathetic. She suffered with Christ in that film you just watched. *(It was Easter and we had just watched a film about the life of Jesus.)* All the teaching was contained in that film. Christ tried to let the world know. It is such a simple message and yet the hardest task of this side is to get through to the minds of man.

You have had a good day with James and Heather *(my son and daughter - the three of us had been walking in the country).* They have much to teach you. Children are the nearest to God because they have not yet become cynical.

One can learn much from children. The problem comes when they reach maturity and the danger is that they will become embittered with life. But do not dwell on this because all is revealed again on this side. Over here you can see your mistakes and learn from them.

If, however, people could know the truth whilst on Earth they would save much time and suffering in advancing their karma. As we told you previously, you are one of the fortunate ones who are now aware. You now only have to apply your knowledge.

The books you are reading are very good and contain much truth. These truths we will confirm to you in our way in due course. This will help you understand and hopefully others, because we intend to tell the truths in simple language and style which will be easily understood. Sometimes the teachings from this side are too complicated and difficult for the uninitiated to grasp. We will try to keep well away from jargon.

You are the right type of instrument. We can only put thoughts into your head and search your mind for the correct vocabulary. Your mind and thoughts are articulate and suited to modern-day language and understanding. Fortunately, they have not been complicated by highly academic vocational training.

We will explain this further. We refer you to a person you greatly admire, Patrick Moore *(the astronomer)*. Why does he command such interest and respect from ordinary people who find astronomy and science fascinating but incomprehensible? Because he uses language they can understand. He expresses very complicated subjects in a simple way and he has amusing mannerisms. He is brilliant but human. People can admire him and yet laugh at the same time.

We believe that we are able to find in your mind and vocabulary the same simple reasoning and delivery of the highly complicated subject which is normally and usually unbelievable to most Earth minds, though this is changing. Many more people are becoming aware of the truth.

I had to interrupt and ask that I be excused to get a handkerchief.

Yes, go and blow your nose, it's making my eyes water.

. . . confirmation that the discourse was often human and not at all reverent! We continued:

Fortunately in recent years it has not been an offence to spread new ideas and information. In the main, freedom of speech and writing are now prevalent. This means that information can easily be obtained by many people. For centuries this has been stifled by either churches or states, often under pain of death. Superstition is dying. The age of Aquarius is bringing new awareness and knowledge. People will still laugh and be sceptical but they cannot hurt you for teaching and fewer and fewer people will laugh as the experiences of people like you are spread.

We have said enough, we said we would not talk of profound matters but we fall easily into the trap in the wish to spread knowledge. Also even though unwell your mind leads us on.

We will talk next week of serious matters and of course John will speak with you in the meantime. He is quite an artist? Keep meditating and you will see.

Keep well and have love. John, Wilhelm and friends.

15th April

You are a little better today. Your cold is finally passing. This is Wilhelm through John. Now we can continue your teaching.

So, we have discussed the basic law of Karma and now we enlighten you to further truths.

You now understand so much it is difficult to know where to begin. But we will try. You should try to empty your mind of all thoughts. We will pause.

I waited for approximately three or four minutes and then the writing began again.

The situation over here is most difficult for people of Earth plane to grasp. They either disbelieve altogether or have a mistaken concept that it is something deeply occult and frightening, or they go in entirely the opposite direction and pay too much attention to their own spiritual concept.

The spiritual concept is man made. We do not decry this nor argue, if by translating the eternal law of love, people surround it with a spiritual coat. But frankly it is so simple to understand once you start from the utterly new and completely original concept, that is - original in terms of earthly and scientific thinking.

Actually our world is more governed by scientific laws than yours. To us there is nothing mysterious in our existence. It is as normal to us as yours is to you. The very simple truth is that we are people as you are but we live in a different dimension. That seems the simplest way for us to explain it.

Try to forget the earthly concept that life begins with birth and progresses for 60 or 70 years until death. Your concept is that something mysterious then happens and most of you believe, or hope, that some indefinable spirit within you passes onward to some type of heaven or otherwise. This passing-over teaching comes from the true and perfect being and medium Jesus, but unfortunately his words and teachings, though in essence unaltered, have been translated over the centuries into the wrong concept. Also Jesus, although he knew he was a high spirit and knew the divine truths whilst on Earth, was still in a man's body with man's mind and even he had to interpret his inspiration and seeing knowledge in his way.

He did it very well but not perfectly, though his demonstration of love was absolutely perfect, because this came from his spirit. Unfortunately he was hampered by his Earth body and brain in explaining the concept. As stated, this was even more distorted by bigots, zealots and religious factions of one sort or another over centuries.

So then, let's start with the entirely different concept (by orthodox standards) that life does not begin at birth. Life begins on our side of the etheric not yours. Life starts here and continues here eternally. Time has no meaning here, only on the Earth plane is time of consequence. We (and you, all of you) progress here for eons and eons of time. Onwards and upwards improving through the workings of the Karma.

From time to time we have to make a journey onto the Earth plane and into a newly formed body in order to gain experience and learn.

This body in the early stages of a spirit's development is of an animal form and it starts very low. As one learns and gains experience one is raised into higher and higher bodies until, when one has reached a fairly high standard of development one is incarnated into primitive man. Onward goes the progression, repeatedly incarnating into more highly advanced and more highly civilised man until eventually one reaches such stage of development and awareness that the spirit no longer needs to return to Earth in order to gain experience. Finally we reach a stage where one can travel onwards to the truly high planes of existence. Let's pause a while.

Now, all this incarnating is necessary because of the basic laws of existence and progression and the fact that one can progress only through the knowledge and acquisition of love. Only through learning how to love fellow spirit even to the exclusion of one's self can one progress. The acquisition of love knowledge at every stage of development makes one so happy and content that one searches onward and higher to acquire a more perfect awareness of this love. Thus does one progress and only through the trials and difficult problems of Earth life is this love truly tested.

In the early stages of development, in say animal form, one returns to Earth repeatedly and very quickly, but as one progresses to higher levels, the time lapse (by Earth standards) is longer and one can remain here for 500 or 1000 Earth years before returning to Earth. John for instance, has not been back for 500 years and he will soon be ready to return.

So then, if we can lose the concept of life beginning with the birth of a baby on Earth we can begin to grasp reality.

Now, about the scientific aspects. The physical world (your world) is governed by its physical laws. Why should we not have laws which are physical to us, but which cannot be explained by scientists in your world because they cannot know of their existence? They have nothing to relate them to.

A primitive native in South America cannot conceive of, for instance, television, but you take it for granted. The scientists of your world are as ignorant as that primitive native in attempting to grasp the concept of our world, because they have nothing to relate it to. We could if necessary prove the fact if we (or the power above) were so inclined, but then what would be the point? The whole reason for incarnating and learning would be lost.

How is it then that some people on Earth gain the knowledge and indeed can converse in various ways with people over here? Simple.

When your spirit (it is not quite the correct description but it will do for now) incarnates into an earthly body, the intention is that it should not be aware too greatly of the fact of its true life. But that hopefully, it will have a deep subconscious awareness of affinity with the other side, in order that it can receive instruction as it progresses in the Earth body.

For instance, if the Earth body is in trouble the spirit may call for help subconsciously. Often this takes the form of prayer communication. Help is usually given, or guidance, but it does not necessarily follow. It depends on the prayer.

Of course the extent of awareness in people varies tremendously and there are and always have been people on Earth who have a greater awareness than others. It is often a freak of nature that their spirit is not quite so deeply attached to their body, as perhaps is usual.

Such people then, retain some of that ability which is natural in our life, the ability to see into our dimension. These people are generally called a psychic or medium. Often they are bemused or concerned and unable to tell other people because they are afraid of mockery.

Most children when very young retain this power for a while until their spirit is fully absorbed into the physical body. These are the children who tell the stories of seeing people, whom their parents cannot see and therefore are rarely believed. After a while the child ceases to speak to deaf ears and usually the spirit settles into the Earth body with its attendant scepticism.

However, some people retain this power and develop it. This is good for them and they should consider themselves fortunate because they then have insight. Such insight can help them progress far more quickly than normal, mainly because they learn more about the true meaning of love, for this is the message they continue to receive. Always they are informed of the power of love, for the benefit of all who can allow themselves to be consumed by it.

The sad thing is that all religions and civilisations pay lip service to love but few truly serve it, but then you cannot achieve perfection on Earth, only over here and only after inconceivable ages of time has elapsed.

There, I think we have spoken enough tonight. The important message we wish to bring (apart of course from love) is that of concept. Forget the concept of Earth life first - heaven later. It is not true. If you like, it is heaven eternally with occasional experience and learning trips to Earth - just momentary trips in time. If you can accept this (and we now know that you do) then it opens the door of awareness. Progress onwards for the door is now open to you.

Yes, the teaching is finished for tonight.

Keep well. Have no fears, be happy and give love. Wilhelm, John and friends.

22nd April

Once again, the day for Wilhelm's teaching had arrived and I had looked forward to this communication.

It started with some personal messages and business encouragement and I wrote for about five minutes on this. They then asked me to rest for a while and return with a clear mind. I returned to the pen and we began.

Yes, you are ready. The next stage of the instruction concerns the concept of God.

We have said before that God is a state of being, not a person. This is neither true nor false. We put it to you in this manner in order that you discount the orthodox concept of the benign omnipotent person of man image - though this is a nice concept! The most difficult concept to explain is that of God.

God is the highest spirit in the universe. God is the essence of life. God is goodness, light, power and absolute love. God is uncomprehendingly advanced in love that he (for the time being we will say 'he') can allow evil to have its place in the universe, in order that spirit may dwell on such and fight to overcome this evil. Only by facing evil and ceasing to be affected and influenced by evil (which takes a long time) can a spirit understand and comprehend the value of love and the power of that love in assisting the spirit to win through.

Only through such trials and fighting can the spirit gain this love and with it more strength to gain more love and so on. Therefore, God has to allow evil to dwell, otherwise there will be nothing to battle with and spirit would wallow on the lower planes of semi-enlightenment without progressing nearer to God. Can you imagine a spirit so full of love that nothing can deter it from absolute benigness? It cannot commit an evil act or thought. If harmed in the most terrible way it would not retaliate. It would forgive any abuse and continue to pour forth love on its tormentors. Such love is inconceivable on Earth (and almost so on our side). This absolute is God and it is to this that we aspire.

Frankly we do not have certain knowledge of the total concept of God because his plane is so high that we cannot communicate. We can only communicate with the next plane upwards and so on until we are eventually next to God.

Jesus is the highest spirit known to us and he is at present on the 7th level. This is the highest level known to us and we believe that higher than that the spirit becomes totally infused with God. This is why we say that God is a state of being, because once one reaches such height one cannot come again to the Earth planes and one is in such a highly intellectual state that one is infused with what we term 'total spirit'.

At such a state, spirit loses its individuality and becomes fused into the whole. There is no longer need of individuality because there is nothing to learn - nothing to be cleansed from the ego by individual experience. It has all been learned. One has achieved total knowledge and awareness, therefore one is totally with God.

Is therefore God a single spirit who originally was as we . . .? We think not. Perhaps God is the infusion and culmination of many spirits who have made the journey of millions of Earth years, evolving to this state of knowledge. Perhaps this 'divinity' bears its presence over all of us and guides us towards it, nurturing our achievements, failures, trials and learning, until we eventually reach the heights and fuse into its own total knowledge.

A bit deep you might think. We agree. This is the deepest subject of all. It has puzzled and tested man's intellect since time immemorial - on our side also. We on this side (and you when you come over) have more knowledge of the concept, but even we can only learn our experience from our teachers on the planes close to us.

Let us now try to explain more about these planes. The planes are in ascendant order of advancement in love and knowledge, starting with first - the Earth plane. Ascendance can only be gained through love and experience (if you like 'age of spirit') and some advance more quickly than others, for we retain our individuality over here at least on the lower planes.

As one reaches higher it become progressively more difficult to attain the next plane. For instance, it is easier to go from one to two, than from three to four. The greatest advancement, for instance, is to the fifth level. It is more difficult to progress from four to five than from one to four. I hope you understand.

When a spirit is over here it can have insight into the next plane above, but cannot dwell there long because of the light of awareness in that plane, until of course it is ready to make the transition. But by seeing into the beauty of the next plane up, the spirit is usually imbued with the yearning to progress. The spirit cannot be forced into dwelling in a higher plane until it is ready. When it has progressed, the transition will take place naturally and it will pass on. This can take hundreds or thousands of Earth years, but it is inevitable. It is like dying on earth and passing on (not quite the same but this is a good simile), because the next plane up is as different a dimension as ours is to yours.

Once a spirit goes beyond the fourth plane it cannot usually return to the lower Earth planes, but spirits below this level can and they spend much of their time near the Earth plane teaching and serving the lower spirits, who are in need of help and sustenance. Only by such serving and repayment of knowledge and love can they themselves progress higher. This serving takes many forms and one of the forms, is such as dwelling near Earth (your life) and helping the needy, the sick and the poor in spirit, to face their problems. Some such spirits help people who die *(in the physical)* to make the transition across. Some dwell on healing the sick.

Wilhelm, in particular helps the sick in India and has been doing so for some 300 Earth years. He is constantly around the Earth planes of India where there is much suffering. He is a doctor of the spirit over here and was a doctor in some of his lives on Earth. Perhaps he may soon be ready to rest from this for a while and be concerned with his own progression and learning, in his own relatively high plane. When this happens, spirits of a higher progression will refresh him and instruct him and he will contemplate his life thus far, before embarking on his next journey.

We are tiring. Rest for a while.

So then, how can we further explain God to you. We cannot see him - the light of perfection would blind our spirit. We can only be led towards him. We can only serve his wishes, which are so pure in love, thought and concept as to be beyond question. Because, how can one question such benignity. There is nothing to argue with. There is no point of view which may transcend. His teaching and leadership are perfect and we have proved to ourselves by our experience that the more we follow, the more we understand and dwell in his light.

One then can only follow the path - to what? Imagine opening a door into a room and what does one find? - happiness. Then there is another door and we open it - and what? - greater happiness, transcending and obscuring the previous room - and so on and on through the doors. And what unlocks the door - the key is love of fellow spirit, serving and helping of fellow spirit.

The key of love opens the door of knowledge into happiness. Eventually we hope to be able to answer for ourselves the question - who or what is God? By progression we will eventually know, but we all have to find the answer ourselves. It is within the power and ability of all of us to know God.

Until we gain the knowledge we can only conceive of and believe. We believe God is the spirit of life, the guidance, the fusion of perfection. An inadequate explanation? It is all we can give you.

Goodnight and God Bless, Wilhelm, John, Jack and friends.

29th April

Welcome. We are ready to continue the teaching. Tonight we will discuss . . . the difficulty is finding the phrases in your head. We will have to wait until your mind settles. We will talk of light things for a while.

Apparently my friends had felt that my mind was not settled enough to receive their messages and for a few moments they conversed with me with encouragement on personal affairs. They then asked me to meditate for five minutes and return in a more relaxed frame of mind. I did so.

Yes, we are ready and your mind is ready. We can now find the phrases. We have discussed Karma and the concept of God. We have explained the paramount law of love and the object of eternal progression to the heights, through experience, learning and the acquisition of love.

Now let us discuss 'physics' - the scientific laws of our side. The term 'physics' is not quite correct, but it may help you understand and discern from the spiritual and ethereal concepts - the fact that the spirit body in our dimension is equally as physical as your Earth body.

So, you understand that life does not begin

with the birth of a child on Earth, but that life begins on this side. Therefore you have to have a body on this side. In fact you have three.

The first body - the Etheric body, is the lowest body, the one nearest to the Earth (physical) body and the one which connects the higher Astral and Ego bodies to the Earth body. It is merely a link between the Earth body and the Astral. It only serves its purpose whilst you are in Earth incarnation. Shortly after you die (a few days at the most) it is discarded, as it is of no further use.

Some people believe in ghosts. They should, as they are a true and natural (or almost natural) phenomenon. The ghost of a person is really that person's Etheric body (containing the Astral) which has not been discarded when that person has died. Why does this happen? It is difficult to explain but there are various reasons and usually a culmination of various circumstances.

Firstly, if an incarnated spirit is of low intellect this means their Ego (we will dwell on this definition later) is hardly formed or developed. This is not a reflection on them. It merely means they are a young spirit and they require much more time for progression and development. But it can, under certain circumstances, for a while hold them back on the Earth planes after they have died.

The reason is that they have not yet had insight

into and been made aware of the beauty and fulfil-
ment of the higher planes. It is not their fault, they
have merely not had the time to progress and gain
the will to search onward. Therefore they are quite
happy to dwell near the Earth and alongside familiar surroundings, usually pleasantly whiling away
their time enjoying the experiences of others still on
Earth.

These are friendly, fairly happy, but unenlightened ghosts. Eventually, however, they will glimpse
further into our dimension and begin to educate
themselves and search for higher experience. As
soon as they show the inclination (and they always
do, eventually), we then raise them up and begin
their instruction.

In the meantime, under certain circumstances
they can be glimpsed in a form equitable with their
Earth body and appearance, because remember, the
Etheric body is the link and the duplicate of the
Earth body. Remember also they are young spirits
and their Astral body is little developed and their
Ego body hardly, if at all. They can dwell near Earth
for a few hundred years but it is most unusual for
them to remain in ignorance for more than about
three or four hundred years.

There are, however. more highly developed
spirits who remain near Earth in this etheric body
for different reasons. They remain for only a short

time, perhaps a week or two, sometimes a little longer. Unfortunately these are the people who may have died a violent or unexpected death. They may have been wrenched from their body painfully and in suffering. They remain in a state of shock for a while and literally do not know they have died.

Usually when a person is coming to the end of their life someone here is waiting to bring them across and to take care of them and to explain to them. It is usually a previous relative who does this because the person will then know that they have really died. But if someone dies unexpectedly in a strange place it can take a while for us to reach them and they can wander (often disbelieving of their death) near the Earth plane. Generally speaking, however, they do not stay long.

These are the major reasons for the ghost phenomena and except under very unusual circumstances they really cannot cause harm to physical beings. There are some of low intellect who are mischievous and these are the poltergeists, but even they are really harmless if you are not afraid. Fear is of more harm to people than anything else. Understanding banishes fear.

As a spirit progresses then it develops its second body - the Astral body. This is the body of emotion. This is the body which feels and gives love, registers hurt when it is afflicted by such emotions as hate. It is in effect the real body of the spirit. It contains everything and registers everything but the intellect. Without the intellect it is incomplete but it is only through the Astral development that the body can acquire and develop the intellect - the karma progression. When the spirit incarnates into the physical it first has to acquire the Etheric body in order to fuse the life, but when it leaves the physical at death it generally quickly discards the Etheric of no further use, but not the Astral.

The third body and the highest is the Ego. This should not be confused with the 'conscious ego' whereby a person can have an extremely high opinion of themselves. The Ego body is not really a body at all, it is the intellect. It is the mind of the spirit. It is the final manifestation of learning. As the spirit (Astral) becomes more developed through purification of emotion by karma, so the Ego develops. The Ego rationalises the thought of the Astral. It interprets the experience and stores the knowledge. The greater the experience, the more the Ego is developed. The Ego is the body which learns and eventually understands the law of Cause and Effect. The more it understands, the more it interprets and leads the emotion of the Astral until its reasoning banishes all fear, hurtfulness and badness of spirit from the Astral. Then can the two progress onward to the truly high planes.

It is believed that the Ego will eventually discard the Astral as of no further use. That once the spirit is of such high state of development, knowledge and understanding that it becomes pure Ego and intellect. That it gains the ultimate - the all-seeing knowledge.

We cannot see high enough therefore we can only conceive, but I (Wilhelm) doubt this. I cannot believe that the emotional part would ever be discarded, because this is the part which registers the love in order that progression can be made. I find it inconceivable that it could discard the measure of its advancement.

But it is only when we reach the truly high planes that we will be given the knowledge. The knowledge of the total Universe. Whatever is the pure ultimate, undoubtedly the higher the spirit the greater its love and the love and intellect of such high spirits is total. Jesus is your example.

Remember, the world on our side is physical to us. Try to discount any concept of ghostly phantoms. Try to conceive of it in the following manner. You in the physical world have a physical body of flesh and a brain which motivates it.

We have our 'physical' body of the Astral, with the Ego intellect infused into it. The world on this side is very real. It is only a different dimension - probably in the interpretation of Earth scientific thinking you could conceive it as a fifth dimension. The fourth dimension (time) exists only with you. Time is here now. Tomorrow is now. Life is eternal.

Goodnight, love and happiness to you. Wilhelm, John, Jack and friends.

6th May

As usual my friends started by talking of light and personal matters, as was now their habit. I believe it is because when I first approach the writing table my mind is still on the previous immediate experience, perhaps television for instance or is still full of thoughts of the normal working day or week. They tend to move the pen for a page or two discussing my own personal life and then as was usual asked me to rest for a few minutes and come back. I did so and returned after five minutes.

Yes you are ready. We have talked of many things and you now have the basic concept. We will now talk generally of many more things and fill in a few gaps.

Our motives thus far have been to give you an initial grasp of the matter without worrying too much about strict accuracy and overlooking apparent contradictions. We could not be too pedantic because we would not have got the message through.

Feel free now to ask questions if you wish. It will be of help to us in explaining further.

Do you wish me to begin with a question? I asked.

No, we will begin the teaching but you may interrupt with questions.

We have stated that the world here is very real. This is true but we have great affinity with Earth and human life because (apart from the fact that all humans bear the spirit of us) we ourselves are governed by the physical laws of the planets, which are of course governed by the laws of the Universe. These particular laws are not apparent to man but they work in much the same way. Just as man can only exist on Earth and can merely move from A to B in space journeying to such planets, so our existence is centred around planets, one of which is Earth. The 'physical' environments on planets such as Earth are our homes and we can only exist in close proximity to such planets. We can, however, travel (faster than the speed of light) between planets, but we cannot exist in the vacuum of space. Nor can any being or matter that we are aware of.

All life or matter which is established, is centred around planets and anything which is not, is merely moving rapidly between them - until established. Nothing (even a meteor) can exist statically between planets without attaching itself to another object (planet or moon) of much larger and greater significance than itself.

The Earth and its moon are attached to the Sun. The Sun motivates its own solar system, but the Sun itself and the Solar System are attached to, integrated with and influenced by much larger constellations - and so throughout space and eternity - each body motivating lesser bodies and being influenced by greater bodies. The smaller are dependent on the larger. The younger dependent on the older - natural law.

So it is with the spirit, the younger influenced by and dependent on the higher. The higher controlling and leading the lower towards itself. The highest spirit leading all to its own perfection. You see how we always come back to the concept of spirits' eternal progression to the higher God perfection, through love and learning? This is because the natural laws cannot be gainsaid.

So then, we exist in proximity to the planets and cannot exist in space but can only move through space. Fortunately we are not subject to human physical laws. We do not need to breathe etc. and therefore we are not restricted to Earth.

We exist around Earth, Venus, Mars, Saturn etc. Do you understand? Do you grasp this? The environment of Venus is not hostile to us because we are not subject to the same physical laws. Such and other planets in the Solar System are perfectly acceptable places, in our dimension. Earth's physical laws have no effect on us. We can move through the noxious gasses of Venus just as we can move through stone walls because in our dimension they do not exist. Interesting isn't it?

Nor are we restricted to the Solar System. There is life throughout the Universe, both physical as on Earth and in our dimension, but of course there is much more life in our dimension than in yours. Don't forget it is still your dimension when you come over, but by discerning it in this manner we hope you will grasp it more readily. For life to develop as on Earth in your dimension, particular evolutionary circumstances have to prevail. The Earth is the only planet in the Solar System to contain life as you know it, but there are many (millions) of other planets which contain life of a similar nature. This is fortunate and probably ordained because such environment and states are necessary for incarnate evolution and learning.

Would you believe that one can evolve and learn more in one Earth life than in centuries over here? Why? Because it is only on Earth that love is really tested. Over here it is much easier to be kind, loving and considerate. There are not the same pressures here. Life here can be very easy if the spirit wishes it. It really is what you make. But in order to progress you must purify the spirit of all evil and only through trial can this be done. However, we must not repeat ourselves. You have already learned this.

It is only when one begins to examine the concept of spirit in relationship to the Universe, that one begins to appreciate the order of things. Perhaps now you can more appreciate our insistence that 'space and science' are of equal significance in our existence as is the spiritual concept. More so in fact, because the only similarity between the true concept of afterlife and Man's religious concept and the only part of Christ's and others' teachings which have been grasped, is the law and effect of love.

Are there physical beings in space venturing from their own planets and visiting Earth? Of course there are. Visitors from space are with you now. They are constantly encircling and landing on Earth. It happens every day and in almost every location. Neither do they come from one place, they come from many different planets and different systems light years away.

They are centuries, often thousands of centuries ahead of Earth in development. Earth people are children to them. Earth people to them are as primitive man is to your most learned professors. Uneducated, unknowledgeable, undeveloped.

These people have been visiting Earth from time to time purely from interest and often as they are passing through the Solar System to other places. They occasionally make contact but not often because they know that Earth people cannot accept the phenomena (some could!). They are more aware of the laws of the Universe and they accept that they cannot interfere with Earth's development. Man must find his own way to their state of knowledge.

They might be more tempted to give man insight but they are afraid of the effect it would have. Earth's civilisation is not ready yet. If they landed and approached in peace, Earth Governments would be afraid and hostile. They observe the stupidity of unenlightened man in pursuit of destruction and they do not care to be involved.

But they come and they watch and they hope that by their presence, a few of the enlightened people who are privileged to 'glimpse' them, might be able to eventually prevail on society to accept the unbelievable and examine their presence seriously, without fear.

O.K. We understand you have to go. This is sufficient food for thought. We will speak further next week.

Love, Wilhelm, John, Jack and friends.

I had had to close the teaching because I had to collect my daughter from a school concert. I asked if I could continue later in the evening or the following evening but they firmly said no, that they would speak to me on the following Friday. I was a little disappointed because the instruction was particularly interesting and absorbing, but I had now begun to accept that all would eventually be revealed in their own way. Furthermore, I was now firmly of the opinion that they really did know best.

13th May

Last week we talked of the spirit relationship with the Universe and of its 'physical' place in the environment. We will continue and extend on this theme.

So the spirit exists in its own dimension, which is different to the Earth physical, but this dimension is interspersed with the Earth physical. It is not another place, it is 'amongst', so to speak. You continually move and pass through our dimension and we through yours. Except in unusual psychic circumstances you cannot perceive ours. You see right through us. We are completely transparent and non-existent to you and yet we exist.

We have a 'physical' appearance, we have places in which to abide. We do not use the same senses as your physical, such as eating and bodily functions. We do not smell the same odours etc. but we 'experience'. We have sight, though not through physical eyes. We have love for each other though not through sexual bodily functions. We experience emotion though we cannot feel physical pain as you know it. Pain is experienced by us but is of a different nature. It is hard to define for you, but for instance, if serenity is interrupted by anger then pain is actually felt by the receiver of the anger. But it is pain of 'spirit'. Pain of 'mind'. We feel sorrow, happiness, love and all the human emotions, but our response to them is much more intense, because we are more preoccupied with emotion than material wellbeing.

This is because we have no material necessity. Our life here is what we make it. We have everything we need to exist and true happiness can only come through serenity and development of spirit and intellect.

This then is the constant state throughout the Universe, spirit incarnating with many civilisations where planets can support life. But whilst life on a planet may vary and may come and go in evolution and degree of development, the law and state of spirit between incarnation is constant. Civilisations in other parts of the Universe may be eons in advance of Earth in development and technology, but their people's spirits are not necessarily so, because their spirits come and go in their own dimension and as usual 'physical planet civilisations' have limited knowledge of this side.

It is a strange anomaly that the more advanced the Earth civilisation generally, the less in tune are its people with the spirit and with our dimension. This unfortunately is because the god-science takes over from the true God and that which cannot be scientifically proven of course does not exist with such men of science and learning. As you know we are not allowed and it is not our volition to give proof. As we have stated previously this would only undermine the whole reason for incarnation and learning. Only when one looks for guidance with an open mind, or truly asks for help, is insight forth-coming. The faith has to be triggered by the being.

You ask, does the spirit incarnate only into civilisations on one planet? We can tell you, no.

Generally until the spirit becomes older and more advanced it remains near its early environ-ment, but as it advances it is allowed to experience other environments and planets. Also, for the bene-fit of its learning it may be desirable that it is born into various world civilisations just as it may be born into various civilisations on Earth.

We think it is time you now learned something about yourself. Tonight you have earned a treat by your application to your emotional problems. We will tell you something about your past incarna-tions. We can feel you are excited and it gives us pleasure.

John has told you about your previous life in medieval France. You have had two lives since then, but they were relatively unimportant. On your last visit you came to learn a specific experience and you only stayed a short time, approximately 23 years.

Prior to your life in France with John and myself you had dwelled on our side for many hundreds of years. This was because you are an old spirit and had experienced many incarnations. You had much important work to do on this side and it was not necessary for you to come over to Earth for some time.

Your life on Earth, previous to medieval France was during the ascendance of the Roman Empire and you were a person of high birth in the Roman civilisation. You and I (Wilhelm) were also together in that life. I was a senator and your father was also of the senate. You were a very good person during that life and disapproved of much that passed for civilisation. You lived during the time of Tiberius. He was not a very good emperor, but then hardly any emperor was good during this period in Roman history.

You also lived in ancient Greece some 2,000 years before Christ was born and again your path crossed with Wilhelm, who during that particular life was your father. Wilhelm is an older spirit than you and has been a great influence on you during many lives.

You are a particularly political person (you know this) and generally your political and social instinct has shown its presence in many of your lives, often in companionship and mutual instincts with Wilhelm.

But now for the most interesting information.

You lived and had numerous incarnations during the Atlantean period of ascendancy on Earth. This was the greatest period of achievement on Earth and it was unfortunate that the terrific catastrophe took place when it did, because it truly retarded Earth's development.

During this period, approximately 15,000 years ago, the Earth was divided into two distinct ethnic groups - the Atlanteans, highly advanced, educated and beautiful people and the primitives (remember do not denigrate primitives as they are only young spirits).

The Atlantean population was the smaller, approximately 200 million but it was completely contained in what was then the civilised part of the Earth, stretching from northern Europe to the South Atlantic, in fact where the Atlantic is now situated. This was not at the time all ocean, it contained an island continental strip approximately 4,000 miles longitude and 1,000 miles wide.

If the Atlanteans had a fault, it was that they contained themselves in this elite location and in an elite environment, but then they truly were elite. But it must be said in their favour that whilst they did not attempt to greatly educate and improve other civilisations on Earth to their state of advancement, neither did they exploit them nor make war. Nor did they dominate them even though they had the power. They were technically and aesthetically very advanced, but they were also peace loving people.

They had mastered the art of gracious and benevolent living, that is benevolent amongst themselves. Crime was almost unknown. Reason prevailed over all and yet they could not save themselves, because when the Earth shifted on its axis there was practically no warning. Almost the whole of the race was wiped out during the reformation of the continent.

The survivors created two great civilisations (by historical Earth standards) and they began to rebuild back to their previous state. One of these civilisations was in South America and the other on the northern continent of Africa near the Mediterranean, which was reformed with the catastrophe. From these Atlantean societies descended the Ancient Egyptians and the Ancient American races of the Aztecs and Incas.

But with the progression of time the civilisations declined. The Atlantean survivors being few, had found it necessary to interbreed with the local, less advanced native populations and due to customs and doctrines over the centuries the impetus which had been lost with the catastrophe was never regained.

If we can draw a parallel for you. Imagine a computer programmer shipwrecked on an island and living his life amongst unsophisticated natives.

Whilst he would do his best to improve their civilisation with his knowledge and ability, he would be fighting a losing battle. He might pass some of his knowledge on to his children and grandchildren and so on, but eventually his civilised knowledge would become hearsay and his teachings no longer understood. The ethnic reality would take over from the intellectual memory and teachings.

So it was with the Atlanteans. They could never reproduce their civilisation because the civilisations they had entered had to gain the vast knowledge through their own experience. If you like, you cannot teach a ten-year-old how to split the atom and perhaps only one in a million would understand the theory when he reached the age of 30. You understand?

But the Atlanteans left many traces of their civilisation and much of their learning was passed on, particularly to the Ancient Egyptian races. We will leave you with one profound piece of information concerning this.

Do you really think that the Pyramids were built by the Egyptians as tombs for their kings? We find it amusing that so-called scientific and learned man does not yet conceive of the true reason for these achievements, which have never been surpassed by man, with all his scientific advancement.

The Pyramids were not built 4,000 years ago,

but more than 10,000 years ago. They were built in numerous parts of the Earth and in varying proportions, but the finest examples are in Egypt.

They were built by the descendants of the Atlanteans to an amazing precision of engineering and the highest conceivable state of indestructibility. Why? As libraries and store houses for their knowledge. They knew they were fighting a losing battle to civilise the world. Man's inherent bent for destruction and factional antagonism was overcoming the flower of civilisation. They wished their knowledge to be stored in such a manner that it could only be regained by future civilisations who hopefully would have gained the knowledge to understand the complexity of the structured libraries and open them.

And what happened? Unfortunately, the Ancient Egyptians with sufficient education and knowledge eventually opened the Pyramids and took out the vast data, most of which they could not understand. As time progressed the kings thought they would be most suitable for tombs for their own elite burial and this is why present-day Earth thinking is muddled as to the original purpose of the Pyramids. The learned minds of present-day Earth have 'seen wood and guessed trees' - they could not be further from the truth. The Pyramids were there before the Egyptian Kings. The knowledge or much of it was retained for centuries by the Egyptians, but gradually through ignorance the records eroded or were destroyed.

It was a terrible waste and mankind is having to re-learn all over again. It is a pity because all the present-day wonders of science had been learned and far surpassed by the Atlanteans. They had left the aeroplane behind, television was unnecessary to them - a primitive means of communication. The power source of their transportation, which would make present-day jets and rockets obsolete, has not yet been reinvented or discovered - the power of gravity, or the utilisation of gravity. It is no use explaining this further, you could not begin to understand.

So you had many incarnations in Atlantis and none of them more important than your Earth experiences amongst lesser races, because all incarnation is for a specific purpose of learning. Those who have experienced the heights have also experienced the depths, or will do so. It is the law of Karma, the law of progression, through learning and love.

Goodnight and God Bless, Wilhelm, John, Jack and friends.

20th May

Once again my friends started with a mental exercise in order to relax my mind, consisting of general discussion and writings on personal matters. After a few minutes they recommenced the teachings.

You are ready to learn more about yourself. We told you last week about some of your lives in Ancient Rome, Greece and Atlantis. We will tell you tonight about your experiences in Atlantis.

You were incarnated many times as an Atlantean, because as we said you are an old spirit. You developed great powers in Earth body as an Atlantean, some of which you retain dormant and are not aware of.

The Atlanteans were very developed spiritually and they had, as a race, come to accept completely the concept of after (and before) life with incarnation. They had total knowledge of the 'law' and therefore naturally lived by its high principles and so developed their awareness whilst in Earth body.

It is for this reason and because of this dormant knowledge that we are able to get through to you and you have readily opened your mind to us.

The Atlanteans, because they fully accepted the phenomena, practised and developed the art of living by and in accordance with the natural laws. Therefore they had little sickness and where sickness occurred they knew it was caused by the spirit of the person and therefore concentrated on healing the mind and spirit. They had little requirement for orthodox doctoring as you know it, though their physical doctors were far more advanced in medicine than today on earth.

The Atlantean doctor was as much of spiritual and 'psychiatric' ability as of physical and only occasionally was surgery needed. People lived to great ages - 130 years would be average, 150/160 was not uncommon.

Another ability, which was developed from a very young age, indeed from birth, was thought transmission. Just as we in our world are able to transmit and pick up thoughts instantaneously over great distances and just as we are able to communicate with you and vice versa, practically all Atlanteans could do this.

You can draw a parallel with this in present-day Earth literacy. Very few people in the Western World cannot read or write. Only people of either lesser intellect (no disrespect, love them), or who unfortunately have been denied the education or have some kind of learning disability, are illiterate. So with the power of thought transmission with the Atlanteans. Only similarly few deprived people could not do this because most learned it from birth, just as reading and writing takes place in your schools.

Can you now understand how their knowledge and development was boundless? Imagine their teachers instructing the young. They had no need to describe and painfully instruct in teaching, they merely placed their thought pictures or ideas or concepts in the student's head and awareness was apparent. A child or any person could learn more in a day than you could learn in a week. You can travel today to America in hours, yet it used to take weeks. You understand? So it was with knowledge.

But it only came with centuries of spiritual development and yet the seed is with the people of Earth now, as it is in people like you and other psychics. If only more people's minds could be opened. It is sad. It seems that for centuries man's mind has been closed by various regimes, 'civilisations', bigots etc. when the flower is there and will bloom if given the chance.

However, the Western World is encouraging, there is much freedom of thought. With all its material preoccupation the World has much tolerance of action and mind in certain places. You are fortunate in your country that this is so, because if you can retain this freedom more people will enquire and learn. Development will progress and once it gathers momentum it can be rapid. The problem is man's shortcomings as a corporate society. It is often tragic that the people of violent mind take control of societies and stifle freedom and dignity.

You now have insight into how particular spirit personalities and traits can be nourished or harmed. For instance one person could 'die' in the army or any disciplined environment and flower in a free and emancipated environment, and yet this person could perhaps cope without so much love around him. We are all different. One person may need more love than the next, but could cope with practicalities much better. It is possible to win an argument with your neighbour, but lose a contract to them. We are all so different, but no one can give too much love, some can just cope better than others with less.

Rest a while.

I don't know whether they were tired or whether they felt that I was tired but I rested for approximately ten minutes and then continued.

Yes, back to your Atlantean latent ability. We are a little disappointed (not very) at your lack of application to meditation because the ability is there dormant within you.

We understand the reason. We know your mind is very active with business and you lead a very full life. We are prepared to wait until you are ready but we recommend that you attempt to set aside a few minutes each day to contemplate because it will be so good for your spirit. We do not mean reflective thought, which you do often. We mean true meditation. It takes time to develop the gift but it is truly worthwhile. With true deep meditation the mind receives more refreshment in a very short time than in a whole week of sleep. In a matter of a few months of meditating for twenty minutes each day you would have the ability of a guru. It is there in you waiting to be developed.

You can do this automatic writing and yet your mind is only minutely open to us. Can you appreciate what is within your capabilities?

We look forward to your long delayed holiday when you will hopefully truly relax. We will then truly discourse with you and hopefully open you completely.

Remember, 10,000 years ago you could read people's minds across the world. You could transmit a complete picture to others with your mind. You can now communicate and summon us from great distances with only a flash of thought.

Consider this.

Goodnight with love, Wilhelm, John, Jack and friends.

28th May - Saturday

I had been unable to talk to my friends on the Friday and so our writing had been postponed until the Saturday. I had been playing cricket all day and being a very average second team cricketer, as often happened I had not scored many runs and was a little despondent.

Their opening remarks are an indication of their humour from time to time and their application to logic in every situation. They felt that I was a little uptight and for five minutes they wished to relax me. This took the form of having me freehand draw lines across the page to start with and then the following personal communication came through.

This is to relax you. It is a good way to get your mind free from Earth. You are not in a very positive mood tonight. Is it because you did not bat well? We think so, but it will soon pass.

You take everything you do and attempt to do seriously, so you are disappointed if you don't reach your expectations. It is a wise man who knowing his limitations can abide with them. You know your limitations but refuse to accept them. So then, you cannot be too disappointed if you only reach your own expectations.

Why should you exceed what you know is probable? The possible only happens occasionally and the probable happens more frequently. You will probably not bat well each week and possibly bat well now and again. See your spirit is rising already because you have humour and can see reason. Good, now you are ready.

As usual they had put me in a good frame of mind and the writings commenced.

We promised to explain the facts of the astrology chart to you and we will start with this.

Man over the centuries has perceived that the time of year a person is born has a bearing on his personality. Very few have grasped why and great confusion has arisen. This is because they 'see wood and guess trees', without delving deeper into the phenomenon and trying to find out why. They know the effect but do not seek the cause.

Great study has taken place and much knowledge has been handed down from the ancients. But all that has happened is that man has used the position of the stars and planets at birth as a measure of man's personality. Man's personality has nothing to do with the stars. It is to do with the kind of person he is and the personality trait definitely is different in each person and the type of personality dictates when a person will be born, or rather, incarnated.

For instance, you think you are Sagittarius or Capricorn, depending on which periodical you read! It matters not. However, people born at the same time as you have general similar personality traits as you and are very different in temperament to say a Cancerian or Pisces. But even a Capricorn varies within days or even hours of birth. By that we mean that a person born on the first of the month, will differ considerably from one born on the fifth, though they be of the same sign. Both will be quite similar in personality but very different in personality from a person born three months earlier or later.

The names of the signs, for instance Cancer - the crab etc. are almost irrelevant and as stated so are the planets. They are merely used by man to denote and indicate and to tie a label on the type of personality. One could just as easily have a number commencing with 1 and then say that people from 1 to 30 are all a similar type of person. This would be true. But it so happens that the calendar is a more useful measure because the stars and planets are fairly constant, always reappearing either annually or periodically in the same constellations and positions relative to the earth. Therefore one can depict, that if one is born in a certain month and the moon and sun were in a certain position, then the person will be of such a personality which is usual with that formula. This is correct but the stars do not direct this, they are only the measure, the yardstick so to speak.

It is to do with the personality of the spirit and the personality and development of the spirit dictates when they are incarnated.

As the personality, learning and intellect advances in the spirit, so then the 'star type' changes, because it is a fact that certain 'star types' (birth times), are more advanced than others and there are lower star types in the zodiac as well as higher. Do not think for a moment that we would indicate to you which are higher and which are lower. There are many things we will tell but this is forbidden and we think you will understand why.

If we indicated to you (and others like you) which were the higher and lower intellect 'star signs' and if such knowledge was accepted, then people could develop awful inferiority complexes, or indeed superiority complexes and this would be undesirable. Further it would be unnecessary and somewhat irrelevant because it is to do with progression and as you know, everyone starts with a low intellect and progresses upwards. It is no reflection that they are born under one of the lower star signs because they have to learn, and anyone born under a higher star sign has progressed and learned further - simply, an older spirit.

So if you wish to know which are the highest 'star signs' you will have to study and reason it out for yourself and it can be done.

Although there are very definite personality traits in people, which are relevant to their birthdays, this is not absolute. Whilst the personality dictates the time of birth and therefore the 'star sign', the character develops on Earth, or otherwise, depending on many factors, such as environment, upbringing and various other circumstances. Therefore through astrology one can only generalise on the type of person. The character of similar star signs will change depending on the foregoing influences.

To illustrate further, let us take Cancer. Such people are generally somewhat introvert, with need of love and able to give much love. They tend to be a little anxious. But Cancerians (like everyone) can be very good or very bad people, depending on other circumstances in their life on Earth and on their experiences in past incarnations. But what will be constant, is their general personality. Even though they have become very successful, very happy and well adjusted, they will still be anxious people in their deep self, probably hidden from the world.

So then, the personality depicts the time of birth and man has shown the ingenuity (some of man) to measure this by the stars. But the stars have no bearing on the matter.

You for instance, born in December, could not have been born in June or May. Had you been conceived a month earlier or later, another personality would have entered the body within your mother's body and you would have entered into a child of a different family in order to be born at the time ordained.

We will give you a little further information in respect of personality at birth. Whilst we will not generally discriminate for you, we will tell you that people born at the time of Jesus are of high intellect and spiritual advancement. They are spirits of relatively high plane. We can tell you this because Jesus was not born on the 25th December, so you can still guess!

But we will not tell you of the other signs and dates and you cannot reconcile it by strict chronology of the calendar. Do not think that January is low and December is high. It is not so simple, nor is it strictly governed from the 22nd of one month to the 21st of the next month. The astrologers are not quite correct here. Further there are variations within a few days. Whilst a person born on the 1st of the month will be of similar personality to one born on the 5th, they may differ in many other ways. One may be spiritually very high in say love but low in reason. The other may be average in spiritual love but very high in reason. There are tremendous variations, but be assured the general personality is fairly constant.

It is for this reason that we regret that some of Earth's scientists miss the truth in their search for intelligence and personality traits through genetics, and we will enlighten you here.

The parents' intelligence has no influence, nor responsibility for the intelligence of their child. Their intellect cannot effect or cause a child of similar intellect to be born to them. It is out of their hands and dependent on the time of birth. The only influence a parent can have is on the character. Influence for good or bad in Earth teaching. Hence the reason why a good businessman of orthodox habits can beget an introvert musician or painter and vice versa, and why a poor manual labourer of average intelligence can father a genius. Often because of circumstances the genius will not flower, but nevertheless it can be there.

This is why people should not be forced into having a particular life or following a particular vocation against their will. They should follow their instinct - their 'star' if you like. Sometimes a musician father will have a son who is also a musician by coincidence and indeed influence, but he should not be disappointed if his son follows an entirely different career in life; and yet people often try to press their opinions and concepts on others - particularly parents. This causes loss of understanding and unhappiness.

The object of life on Earth is to progress in happiness and love, pursuing that which comes naturally and which does not detrimentally affect others. If one can actually help and serve others, then this is a bonus especially at the present time on Earth. Then one can advance dramatically in one incarnation.

Lack of understanding is one of the veils of the world and matters would be much simplified if people would listen to each other and love each other. Here we are, back to the same constant theme. One always comes back to it, the teaching of love.

So, you understand that the genetic theorists are wrong. Neither race, colour, environment nor parents dictate the intellect, because the intellect has been evolving and developing for centuries. Only the character can be influenced or helped - or otherwise, by such considerations. If man could only grasp this truth the world would improve dramatically.

Well this is enough for tonight. Hope you enjoyed this instruction. We will talk next week.

Have love, give love and be happy. Wilhelm, John, Jack and friends, and Bob sends love to Maureen, Mum and you all.

5th June

During the last few weeks I had discovered that as Friday approached I seemed to have a premonition or inkling of some of the subject matter which would be contained in the writings. I suspected that my friends began communicating their thoughts during the day, or hours, prior to the Friday evening. However, on this particular Friday I found that my mind was a complete blank of thoughts or ideas and when I picked up the pen I had absolutely no knowledge or inkling of what would follow.

I knew they were there and ready to begin writing and yet I had this feeling that the instruction would not come through. For this reason I anxiously searched my own thoughts, reaching for a subject and willing the pen to move.

What follows will probably indicate that my suspicions were well founded and that I had not in fact received any subconscious contact or programming during that particular week. The reason was to be evident.

Don't worry, there is nothing in your mind. We have yet to put it there. You have become so familiar that you are trying to anticipate. Try to remember what the first communications were like. You had no idea what was coming, so you did not worry. But now you are searching for our thoughts and there is no need. They will come when we are ready.

We have spoken of many things, now it is time to summarise. You have enough information for the first document and in any event we cannot tell you any more significant and deep facts.

You have learned the basic laws and teachings of the Universe and of creation. Such information can only be extended, and anything further we can tell you would only be a more detailed explanation of what has gone before.

Further, the state and concept of matter on this side is almost impossible for you to grasp. There is no way that we can enable you to really conceive of it because there is nothing within your experience with which it can be compared. A most important consideration for us, is that you, at least, are now aware of things and this gives us great pleasure. This means that one more person on Earth, indeed, one more family, indeed one more group of people, know the truth and will lose much of their normal earthly fears because of this knowledge. Because you will now gradually enlighten others - you are already doing so.

But remember, you cannot force your knowledge on others, they must learn and discover the truth for themselves, but you can help them to open the door. Once a person shows some interest or displays a will to learn you can lead them a little at a time towards knowledge and truth. They will be fortunate, those whom you meet who are seriously interested because you have discovered and can pass on the total concept. You had to find out for yourself, but you were being helped from this side and led towards such people as Betty, who could first raise your interest. Likewise, light the spark.

We are not pretentious in thinking that we have unfolded some great truth that mankind had not been appraised of. The truth has been unfolded many times by many people, more clever, articulate and knowledgeable than we and through people more psychic than you.

But we, together with you, have opened another door - just a chink and together we impart our simple message in simple form. The message can never be told too much. It needs many more people to discover and to tell. By such means perhaps the world will become truly aware and the fear, violence, hate and destruction which is implanted in the minds of much of mankind will diminish.

The teachings will cease now for a while. We feel we have taken up much of your time and we do not wish you to be tied to this exercise each Friday. We do not wish a pleasure to become a toil. Perhaps we will return to the matter in due course and extend on the knowledge imparted thus far. In the meantime, be assured that we are never far away from you. Write with John as and when you wish. Write of simple pleasurable things. Correspond in love and although you may not discuss anything profound, you will still learn many things. John is now and will continue to be your constant companion. But do not doubt that if you need me (Wilhelm), you can call me in seconds and I can be with you from anywhere in the Universe within minutes.

Bob is also constantly around the family, especially around Annie and Maureen. Jack is also near, especially around Nick and there are many others. Fred Tyrell loves you all and watches over his clock (left to Maureen in his will). Donald Thompson and father Dick come from time to time. Grandpa Jack

visits occasionally. Whilst we have been communicating with you we have had a tremendous audience
of people coming and going. People who have
known you and your family in life on Earth, too
numerous to mention all.

For they too are excited and even amazed at the
phenomenon. They too marvel that we can communicate and pass our thoughts on to you, because it is
no mean feat. It is not the simplest of things for us to
achieve. We have to try hard and though many
people do try hard, few succeed.

It is only because you are an old spirit and have
psychic ability, and because of our affinity, that we
have succeeded. People over here are very pleased
to see it happen, but also sad, because many have
tried very hard to reach their loved ones and relieve
their grief, to no avail.

*I then asked if there were any specific messages they
wished me to convey to such people.*

No we do not wish you to pass any specific
messages on. They would be too numerous and
many of the recipients would neither believe nor
appreciate it. But remember if you write the book

your friends and relatives can read it and those who are able to believe and take heart from it will question you and the door will be opened for them. You understand?

Now go on to your next adventure. The joyous adventure of healing the sick. You and Maureen have the ability between you to work the so-called miracles of healing. They are not miracles, they are the normal procedures for people who are aware and believe.

Study, read, gain knowledge and begin to heal. Do not be afraid of failure. Failure does not matter. You will not heal everyone, but you will heal many. The successful healings will more than make up for the failures and in any event all is ordained. You cannot heal unless it is ordained and unless the spirit can be helped.

Finally, please try to stop smoking. We rarely advise, but we have told you before that it is practically the only thing, apart from overworking occasionally, which you do which harms your health. Try to stop or you will reach us earlier than you bargained for and we do not wish you to come here until you have lived your full time, because you enjoy life. You are ordained to live to a good age, so stop messing with cigarettes.

There, how is that for a profound ending. From such marvellous teachings see how low you have brought us.

Love to you and your friends and family there. May you all have love and be happy in your Earth life in the knowledge that we await to help and guide you when your time comes.

Love, love, love, John, Wilhelm, Jack, and many, many friends. Love to Mum and Maureen from Bob.

Thus concluded the first teachings of Wilhelm and John.

POSTSCRIPT

I would like to fulfil the promise I made in the introduction of the writings, to return to the question of advisability of the uninitiated experimenting with the 'glass' or the Ouija Board.

Though I do not consider myself in any way an expert or qualified to advise, I have since learned from the 'other side' that it is not always advisable for people to jump in with both feet and in ignorance, as I did. However, I am given to understand that much depends on the personality of the experimenter.

There seems to be little doubt that when one communicates through the glass, one is acting as an undeveloped medium or channel and the spirit coming through actually temporarily uses one's faculties in some unknown way.

There is little doubt also that not all people on the other side are benign and full of love. A person of ill character does not necessarily immediately shed such character on passing over and there are innumerable spirits dwelling low near the Earth plane bent on mischief. This is caused through the spirit's ignorance and low mentality and often through their aggravation or dissatisfaction with their recent previous earth life. A person who is unaware, or of fearful disposition, might have an unpleasant experience with such spirits.

Indeed just as there are extremely evil people on Earth it must follow that they retain that evil when they pass over and perhaps need a long journey through karma to attain a degree of spiritual wellbeing. I have learned that there are many examples of possession whereby spirits or entities of a negative disposition can take over and dominate a personality. Therefore I cannot recommend the Ouija Board as a vehicle for spiritual advancement. I think there are perhaps better ways of gaining knowledge of one's psychic potential, perhaps through contact with and under guidance of advanced mediums.

One thing I have learned, however, is that the greatest barrier to progression is fear and the greatest help is a positive and optimistic disposition. Fortunately I had no fear in the beginning, through my own ignorance and because of my agnostic inclination. I had no preconceived ideas. I experienced some fear as I progressed forward and as I learned and became aware of what in fact was happening to me I overcame it, through the encouragement of my teachers.

I think therefore it would be fair to speculate that a pessimist by reason of his or her own nature would not be likely to experiment in the first place, and an optimist who would be likely to do so would have nothing to fear by so doing.

My outlook and accordingly my life has now significantly changed. Firstly in so far as I no longer fear death and secondly I have become even more optimistic. I can now personally rationalise why so many people suffer in the world, through no fault of their own and I am able to reconcile the apparent unfairness in life. People have always asked - If there is a God why does he let his people suffer? I now feel that I know the answer. God gives us all free will and it is we who make each other suffer and will continue to do so whilst we progress spiritually through Karma. This has become my truth.

By the end of the writings and after, I developed further along the psychic path. I had for some time been able to pick up the thoughts and expressions from my mentors a fraction before the pen put them down. I then progressed to speaking and hearing directly in my mind and have since that time been able to sit quietly and talk, mostly to John in particular, when I have a problem or I am troubled. It has always been hard for me to discuss this phenomenon with people outside my family and close circle of friends and I can imagine the comments: 'He's talking to spirits now.'

I must stress that when I communicate with Wilhelm and John either through writing or in my mind, I repeatedly question the validity of the communications in order to be assured that they are coming from my mentors and not from my own subconscious. I am always reassured.

Over the years, as the novelty of the phenomenon wore off, I would go for long periods of time without any discourse. Like everyone, from time to time I can become preoccupied with my 'earthly' life and I do not feel the need to continually reinforce my beliefs, which are now well established. I have never lost the ability to communicate with my friends, though after a long lapse it requires a bit of extra concentration and meditation. My mentors never reproach me for losing touch now and then.

Their attitude appears to be that I have free will, that I will use it and what will be will be. They practice what they preach.

However, over the last few years the manuscript has been pulled out of the drawer many times, photocopied and given to people who have shown interest. As a result, it has circulated and been copied again and again and I am told it has given satisfaction, pleasure and solace to many people. I have received many letters and phone calls from people all over the world, either asking me for a copy or wanting to know when it will be published. Photocopies of the original manuscript have even turned up as far away as Australia!

Our elderly Vicar, who died some years ago, came to see me after being given a copy to read. Maureen and I spent many evenings with him and his wife discussing theology (about which I knew little) and I was most gratified if not somewhat amazed when he told me that my manuscript had given him answers to many of his questions and doubts on the life hereafter. Particularly so, because I was not a churchgoer and he was a very good and holy man.

Subsequently his curate, who is also a very fine,

religious person, became a good friend to my wife and I. We also had many discussions on the subject matter of Wilhelm's teachings and he maintained that he had never had the true teachings of Christ better explained.

I hope that this book gives some insight and perhaps understanding to those who are uninitiated. It may also perhaps reinforce the beliefs of people who are. Times have changed in that through the 80s, 90s and into the new Millennium, many more people have searched for knowledge and confirmation of life hereafter and with the concept of Karma.

The scientific 'fraternity' will perhaps never be convinced without absolute 'provable' evidence, but 'proof' can apparently only come with those who themselves have experience. Perhaps someday, proof will be available but I think not. As my mentors have stated, to provide proof would only take away the search for truth through faith and personal endeavour. To remove the trial would be detrimental to karmic progression.

As stated, I hope these and other writings may encourage people who are seeking answers to continue the search. The answers are within oneself. 'Seek and you will find' is perhaps the truest religious epithet. I now believe there is nothing extraordinary in my experience, I was merely lucky in my initiation and I had an open mind to pursue the matter. I now believe that the 'gift', if indeed it is a gift, lies within every person.

Perhaps the reader will consider, that the next time he or she goes to bed with a problem and wakes up with the answer, it might not have been the mind that worked it out, but possibly their friends and mentors on the other side who were able to communicate whilst the mind was at rest and therefore not cluttered with earthly thoughts.

To perceive of this is a beginning.

To be continued . . . .

If you would like to write to Peter Shires,
then address all correspondence to:

FORTUNE BOOKS LTD
FAO Peter Shires
C/O GL Publications
PO Box 168
Leeds LS15 9TJ

or Email:
petershires_fortunebooks@hotmail.com

If you would like more information
write to:
FORTUNE BOOKS LTD
C/O GL Publications
PO Bos 168
Leeds LS15 9TJ
tel: (0113) 260 0010
fax: (0113) 232 6536
Email: fortunebooks@hotmail.com
website: fortunebooksonline.com

BLUE MOTHER EARTH
- An Obsession With Time -

Composed and Produced
by
Nick Shires

AVAILABLE ON CD FOR £10.00 plus postage
($20.00 including postage)

Nick, a great composer in his own right, created **Blue Mother Earth** - a collection of 12 symphonic poems that definitely triggers a sense of wellbeing and a feel of wide open spaces.

'The experience of writing and producing this album has given me proof beyond doubt. I feel happy that I've been able to complete this work and reassured to know that I have been able to do all of this without having to rely on the 'safety net' of location or ambience. Instead I relied upon myself and the power of my Higher Self connection.

If you would like a copy, then please send a cheque (UK only) or credit card details, or a postal/money order to:

Fortune Books Ltd, c/o GL Publications, PO Box 168, Leeds LS15 9TJ, UK

e-mail: fortunebooks@hotmail com
website: fortunebooksonline.com

Price UK £12.00 including postage
Price USA and other $20.00 including postage